# ART NOUVEAU

## POSTERS & GRAPHICS

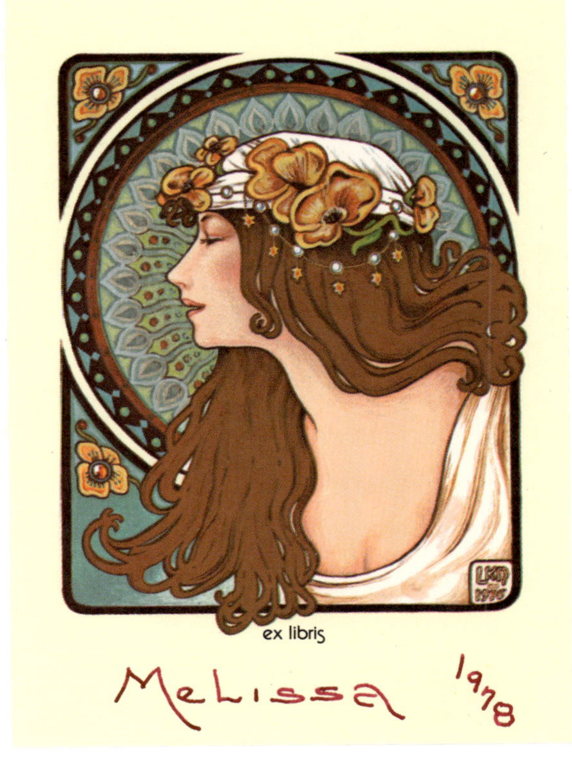

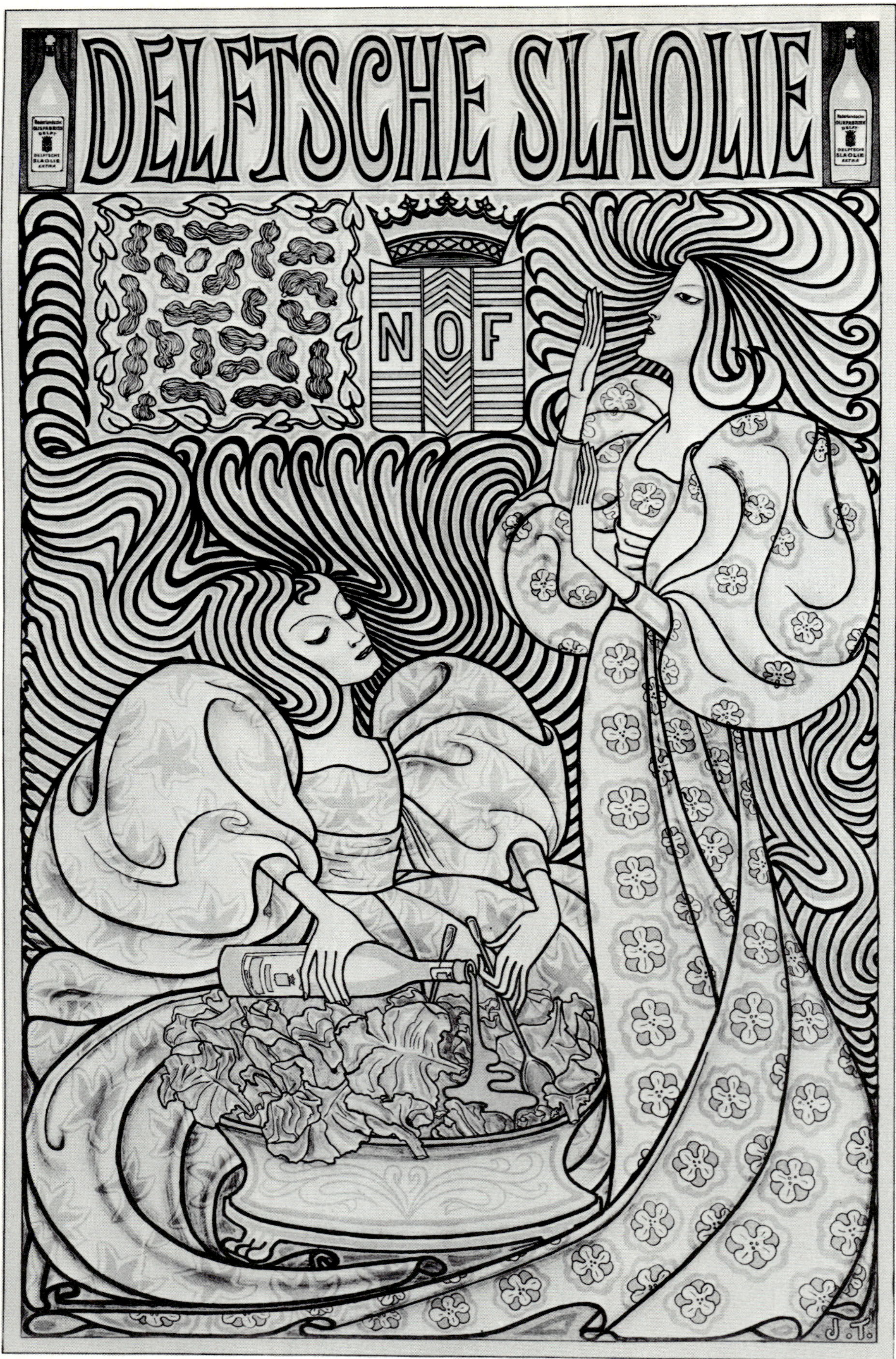


Jan Toorop
*Delftsche Slaolie* 1895

# ART NOUVEAU

## POSTERS & GRAPHICS

ROGER SAINTON

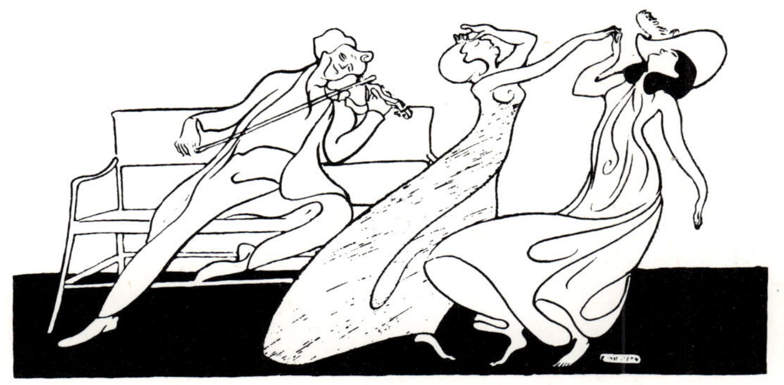

RIZZOLI

**ACKNOWLEDGEMENTS**
We would like to thank the University of Glasgow for permission to reproduce posters in the Mackintosh Collection which appear on pages 84 and 89; Jiri Mucha for permission to reproduce works by his father which appear on pages 53, 54, 55, 56 and 57; and Victor Arwas and Editions Graphiques Gallery for permission to photograph works in their possession from which most illustrations are reproduced.

Published in the United States of America in 1977 by
*RIZZOLI INTERNATIONAL PUBLICATIONS, INC.*
712 Fifth Avenue/New York 10019



Library of Congress Catalog Card Number: 76-51472
ISBN: Hardcover 0-8478 0073-3 Paper 0-8478 0085-7

Printed in Great Britain by
Balding & Mansell Ltd., Wisbech

# INTRODUCTION

The Art Nouveau image is found in its purest form in the poster and on the printed page. Art Nouveau itself is a decorative art which encompasses all aspects of design, yet its antecedents are images on paper, and it is on paper that it is most clearly recognisable in its fully developed form. "Art Nouveau" is frequently thought of as an artistic reaction against historicism, a conscious attempt to break with the past and create a "new art". It was, of course, nothing of the kind. Over the centuries local and national art movements were distinctive because of the dangers, difficulties, and time involved in travelling from one place to another. To study the art of a distant place or to bring one's own to foreign parts was fraught with so many difficulties that it took years for developments and discoveries to filter through from country to country. The propagation of printing, improved transport and the opening of the Far East all contributed to the telescoping of the time span between the introduction of fresh images and their fairly universal availability.

Elements that go into the constitution of the Art Nouveau image were borrowed from a huge variety of sources, the most influential of which was Japanese art. The Far East had long been a useful source of decorative design; the eighteenth century had seen a craze for Chinoiserie which had carried over into the nineteenth. The opening up of the hitherto isolationist Japan as a result of the visit of the American Commodore Matthew C. Perry led, in the 1850s and 1860s, to a flood of Japanese artifacts throughout Europe. Whistler, Bracquemond, Manet and Tissot, were all influenced, as were such Impressionists as Degas and Pissarro. Yet the influence was still alien, not altogether assimilated. Displays of Japanese art in the Paris International Exhibitions of 1867 and 1878, followed by a major exhibition at the Georges Petit Gallery in 1883, were supplemented by a constant stream of articles and books which explored and popularised it. Shops specialising in Japanese art and artifacts opened in Paris and London; on sale were drawings, carvings, silks, arms and armour, hardstones and ivories, and a little later, and most importantly, the woodcut, from the humble actor portrait to the rich surimono, heightened with metallic colours and wafered textures. Increased familiarity meant greater assimilation of Japanese visual techniques and stylisation by European artists. Rather than etch or paint a copy of a Japanese object, they were now composing a European subject using some degree of Japanese visual techniques and stylisation.

Undoubtedly one of the most important steps in the development of Art Nouveau was the publication of *L'Histoire des Quatre Fils Aymon* in 1883. Eugène Grasset (1841-1917), a Swiss artist who had settled in Paris after the Franco-Prussian war of 1870, spent over two years preparing the book for publication. The story itself was a popularised version of a tale of derring-do in the days of the Emperor Charlemagne. The book, however, was the first totally integrated publication, in which the text and illustrations blended and overlay in a dazzling variety of ways: text framed in decorative borders, text printed over part of an illustration, illustration dividing or setting off portions of text, illustration being designed for single as well as double open pages. The illustration was clearly derived from Japanese prints: strong, simple outlines, frozen action, stylised postures and grimaces. Decorative borders and friezes scattered throughout the book used not only Japanese inspired motifs, but also Celtic ones, such as the entrelac, to heighten the medieval feel. Though unsuccessful when published, the book was greatly praised by some critics, and its techniques and style were to filter rapidly into the artistic consciousness of those European artists who were working towards what was to become Art Nouveau.

One of the characteristics of Art Nouveau illustration is the sensuous sinuosity of its line, nervously undulating, curving over itself, twined and intertwined in endless patterns. Often inspired by flower, leaf, or stalk, the line is simplified and abstracted to flat surface pattern. In his use of the fluid, expressive line William Blake may be considered one of the precursors of Art Nouveau. In France and Belgium this line proved an inspiration. Yet in England this aspect of his influence was largely negligible, the efforts of William Morris and his Arts and Crafts movement being directed to the different, if parallel, attempt at 'turning our artists into craftsmen and our craftsmen into artists' in the example of the medieval guilds, but inspired by Socialism, the Gothic vision and Victorian ideals, morals and images. Traces of the sinuous line are found in some of Walter Crane's illustrations, but these are not characteristic, and are found in otherwise static images. The influence of Crane and Morris on the development of Art Nouveau is, rather, in their encouragement to renewal than in the example of their designs.

Within the Arts and Crafts movement the work of the Century Guild and, in particular, two creations of one of its founders, Arthur Heygate Mackmurdo (1851-1942), are frequently mentioned as an influence on the development of Art Nouveau. These are a chair designed in 1881 and the title page for his book on *Wren's City Churches* in 1883. The chair, known from an illustration in *The Studio*, is heavy, solid and stodgy, yet its wooden back is cut in an extraordinary fretwork floral pattern with swirling intertwined stalks. The title page has a similar design of swirling asymmetrical stalk curves winding in flame-like flower heads. Both are pure Art Nouveau. Both are aberrations in Mackmurdo's work without influence or development in either his work or in that of the other Arts and Crafts designers, executed in the course of providing patterns for botanical study, and unrecognised as distinctive by their creators; they certainly occur in the work of Christopher Dresser.

William Morris published the first book of his Kelmscott Press in 1891 in an attempt at renewing the art of printing. Richly patterned borders framed and enclosed the illustrations and the text, which was densely printed and contained elaborate initial letters, giving a medieval feel to the whole. A year later the young Aubrey Beardsley (1872-1898) was commissioned by John M. Dent, to whom he had been introduced by Frederick Evans, the bookseller, to design and illustrate a new edition of Malory's *Le Morte d'Arthur*, which was published in 1893. Beardsley produced some 350 drawings for reproduction by line-block, using the basic Kelmscott page layout of drawn design enclosed within a patterned floral border, but rejecting Morris's classic balance by placing the illustration off centre; making each of the four floral borders of different widths from each other; rejecting the formal naturalism of the Morris floralism in favour of irregular, stylised stalks and tendrils of varying complexity; replacing the classical static illustrations favoured by Burne-Jones by dramatic contrasts of flat black, patterned areas and white spaces, using the possibilities and limitations of the line-block process to create a totally two-dimensional pattern in which the line creates the tension. Morris was furious; he regarded the book as a parody of his own, and considered taking legal action. Beardsley had produced his first Art Nouveau book.

Japanese art, Burne-Jones' illustrations, as well as great admiration for Crivelli and Mantegna went into the formation of Beardsley's line. By the time he illustrated Oscar Wilde's *Salomé*, published by John Lane in 1894, the extremes of extravagance and control were fully developed. *Salomé* had been written in French for Sarah Bernhardt, who intended to perform it at the Palace Theatre in London in 1892, but was prevented by the Lord Chamberlain, acting in his capacity of theatre censor. The Byzantine excesses of the text, rich in sonorous verbiage and Symbolist imagery, appealed to the great French actress and inspired Beardsley to balance the richness of text with elegant drawings in which the large white area is transfixed with a sure, powerful line, each curve swooping like a bird of prey, the decoration reduced to the minimum yet giving off a strongly Oriental flavour, the fine lines balanced by strongly defined areas of dense black. Beardsley was to die at the age of twenty-five, yet in his brief artistic career he managed to produce a large number of drawings whose influence was to penetrate and affect illustration in every country in Europe and the United States.

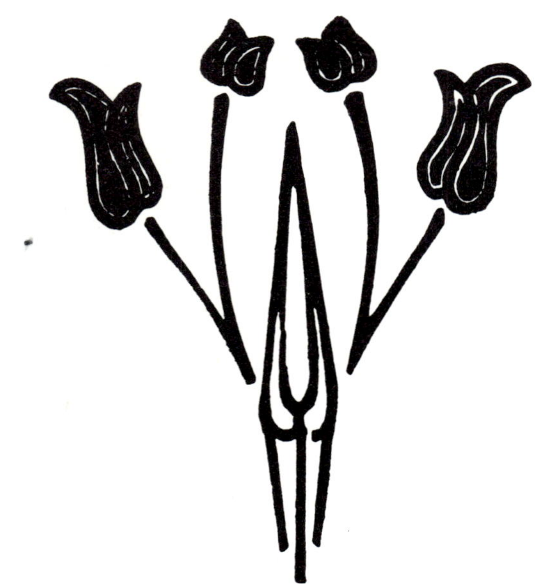

Henry van de Velde
*Illustration*

Parallel with developments in book illustration the poster was evolving towards its own imagery. Jules Chéret (1836-1932), created the modern poster, abandoning the earlier use of poster as provider of information, largely typographic, with small, often irrelevant pictorial areas, in favour of the poster as provider of impact, designed as a whole with a gay, colourful, central figure and a minimum of lettering, all drawn in a style compatible with that of the central figure. Colour was of supreme importance in Chéret, the central figure being seen as strong red, yellow or green blobs from a distance.

From about 1890 Grasset produced an alternative type of poster which was to predominate in Art Nouveau. Chéret's cheerful painterly style was replaced by formal decorative composition, strong outlines and muted colours. His design for Sarah Bernhardt, *Jeanne d'Arc*, was to be the inspiration and basis for Mucha's own posters for that great actress.

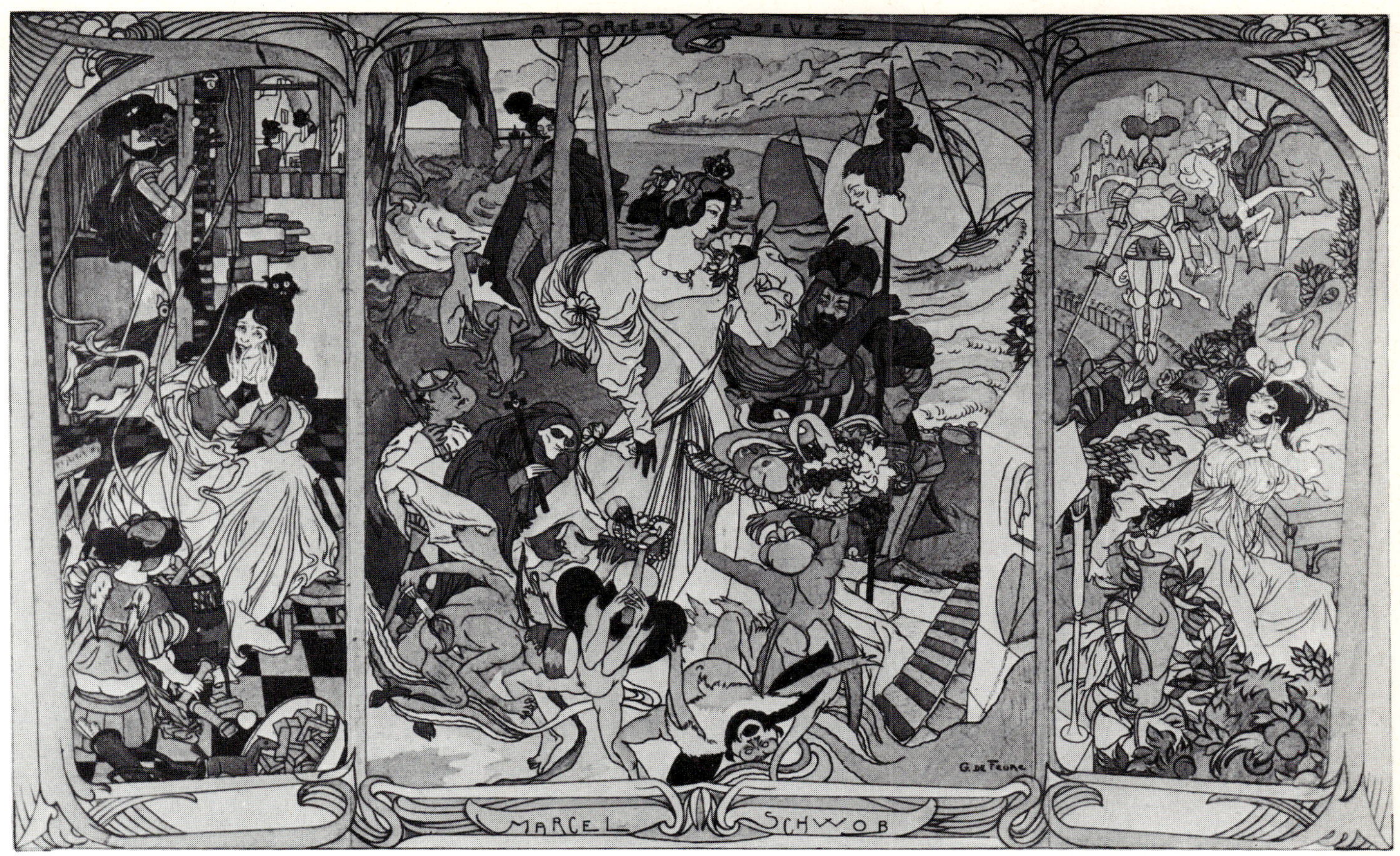


Georges de Feure
*La Porte des Rêves*

Alphonse Maria Mucha (1860-1939), a Czech artist, had travelled to Munich and Vienna before settling in Paris. From 1894 he executed a series of posters for Sarah Bernhardt, as well as designing sets and costumes for her. He also designed posters for a variety of other clients, in addition to designing decorative panels, illustrating books and essaying design in various crafts. Taking Grasset's basic design, he developed it by abstracting and elongating the formal shape of the poster, and filling the spaces surrounding his central figures not only with the Japanese and Celtic motifs favoured by Grasset, but also with Byzantine and esoteric motifs culled from the current interest in magic and witchcraft. Frequently using gold and silver in addition to his usual restrained pallette of colours, Mucha's posters needed to be placed at eye level and needed to be looked at closely. From a distance they were a shapeless blur, with none of the impact of Chéret's posters. Close up they proved an extraordinary draw, and there displayed the full-blown Art Nouveau image. The preferred subject was a woman, with formally arranged hair disposed in continuous outlined patterns which inspired detractors to refer to the style as "noodle" or "macaroni".

This formal patterning derived from Gaugin's ideas via the Nabis, a group of artists which included Denis, Bonnard, Ranson, Sérusier, Ibels, Séguin, Vallotton and Vuillard. Under the combined influence of Japanese imagery, Gaugin's ideas and Symbolist expression, they sought to renew art from its basic sources; as Denis wrote, a picture was, before becoming anything else, 'essentially a flat surface covered with colours assembled in a certain order'. Maurice Denis (1870-1943) himself produced a number of lithographs – mostly book illustrations and some in colour – in which he moved from an Art Nouveau line to a dream-like, soft Symbolist expression. His friend Paul Ranson (1864-1909) produced less in the graphic arts, but his style was even closer to Art Nouveau in a decorative sense, his lithographs bearing a curious resemblance to woodcuts. The Swiss artist Félix Vallotton (1865-1935), on the other hand, produced the quintessential Art Nouveau print, his woodcuts balancing white against black in a dramatic, tension-filled set of patterns.

Georges de Feure (1868-1943) produced some of the most striking Art Nouveau images. Born in Paris of a Dutch father and a French mother, he adopted the name "de Feure" (his real name was Georges Joseph van Sluijters) in the 1890s on his return to Paris after spending some years in the Netherlands and in the Dutch East Indies. He studied with Chéret, but was soon involved in the Symbolist movement, and exhibited at the Salons de la Rose+Croix before joining S. Bing's group of artists when the latter converted his Oriental Art Gallery into a gallery he called *L'Art Nouveau*, thus naming the new movement. de Feure illustrated a number of books, his most striking being Marcel Schwob's *La Porte des Rêves*, in addition to painting and designing ceramics, glass, fabrics, furniture and theatrical costumes and sets. He also produced a number of posters. Symbolist imagery in de Feure was interpreted in an Art Nouveau style, his women – whether nude or elaborately befeathered, behatted, begowned and bejewelled – are the essence of mysterious sophistication, their fine dissipated features hinting at unmentionable erotic delights. His posters

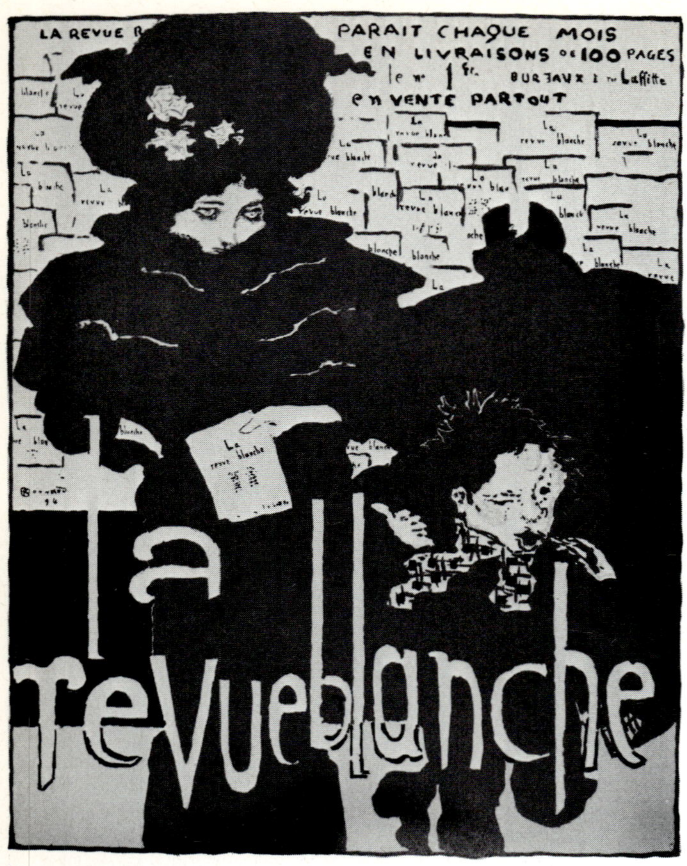


Pierre Bonnard
*La revue blanche* 1894

manage to combine a spiky angularity with swooping curves. The young Henry de Waroquier (1881-1970) produced a few lithographs in an Art Nouveau style (as well as designing some ceramics and other objects) strongly influenced by de Feure before becoming a mainstream painter. Mary Golay, a Swiss painter from Geneva, produced a number of chromolithograph decorative panels strongly influenced by Mucha in various series based on flowers, plants, birds and animals.

Another fine poster artist was Manuel Orazi, who first came to prominence with a poster for Sarah Bernhardt, *Theodora*, 1884. Though enriched with gold, the design of the poster was stodgy and four-square, and it was not until the 1890s that Orazi absorbed the lessons of Grasset, Mucha and de Feure. His poster for the Olympia Theatre's production of *Rêve de Noel* shows the stars Liane de Pougy and Rose Demay, two great beauties of their day, embracing in an equivocal, erotic, yet languid way. His two posters made for the twin theatres at the 1900 Paris Universal Exhibition, Loie Fuller's and the Palais de la Danse, were among his most successful, combining a stylised Art Nouveau woman in the former with various Japanese abstract circular motifs and in the latter with a cascade of circular champagne bubbles, both in soft pastel colours; even his signature was adapted from a Japanese motif. The influence of de Feure is strongest in Orazi's 1905 poster for *La Maison Moderne*, rival gallery to Bing's *Art Nouveau*. Here a hieratic young woman, her fingers, wrist, neck and hair encrusted with jewels sits beside a shelf covered with some of that gallery's *objets d'art*. Orazi himself was to design jewellery for the *Maison Moderne*.

Grasset's pupil, Paul Berthon (1872-1909), was to push the Art Nouveau image further into softness, using less acid tones than Orazi combined with a very strong outline. He frequently adopted Grasset's use of flowers and even of the Japanese formalised diagonal cloud formations in the background, though his clouds and flowers tend to be used like recurrent abstract motifs. His women's hair is utterly transformed into an outlined decorative mass. Mucha's followers included the Toulousain artist Foäche, whose poster for the newspaper *La Dépêche de Toulouse* is here illustrated without the letters, showing the nymph of the Garonne river with many of Mucha's favourite motifs: hair flowing in the breeze, stars, lilies and narcissi, all in pale blues and greens with streaks of gold.

Symbolist artists made frequent forays into Art Nouveau territory, in posters as well as in prints, both as book or magazine illustrations and as separate lithographs, etchings or woodcuts. Symbolism was the content, Art Nouveau the style. *L'Estampe Originale* was the first collection to display this meeting of styles; published in eight quarterly albums starting on March 30th, 1893, the set eventually comprised ninety-five prints, lithographs, etchings, drypoints, aquatints, mezzotints, woodcuts, one wood engraving and one gypsograph, by seventy-four artists. A variety of styles and schools was found in the set, which contained works by professional printmakers such as Braquemond, Chéret, Lepère, Lunois and Rops, and by established artists such as Fantin-Latour, Carrière and Whistler, Gaugin and the Nabis. Art Nouveau prints, or prints with Art Nouveau overtones, were produced by Bonnard, Denis, Maurin, Ranson, Roussel, Vallotton, Auriol, Guilloux, Rachon, Prouvé, Roche, Martin, Delâtre, de Feure, Duez, Grasset, Hermann-Paul, Jossot, Charpentier, Houdard, Ranft and Toulouse-Lautrec. Charpentier, who produced an embossed colour lithograph for the seventh album, also devised a sculptural blind-stamp in the Art Nouveau style for the series.

Inspired by this series, another set of albums was launched in 1897 under the general title of *L'Estampe Moderne*. Whereas *L'Estampe Originale* was published exclusively in an edition of 100 only, *L'Estampe Moderne* was produced as a more popular series, with a *de luxe* edition on simili-japon paper with large margins and first states in black of all the prints on Chine paper limited to 150 numbered sets, and a numbered larger edition of the final states on laid paper with small margins. Not all the prints in this series are original, several of the commissioned artists having chosen to submit drawings or watercolours which were then reproduced in some variant of the collotype process. Nevertheless this set comprised some of the most successful Art Nouveau graphic compositions, and contained several gifts to subscribers, including two colour lithographs by Mucha. Several Symbolist artists who had contributed to *L'Estampe Originale* also contributed to this series, each album of which contained wrappers with a Mucha design.

The cover of the first album of *L'Estampe Originale* was a colour lithograph by Henri de Toulouse-Lautrec (1864-1901). Born at Albi, son of the Count of Toulouse, he was crippled in an accident in his youth, his legs remaining stunted. His early interest in drawing and painting later became an obsessional pursuit. He received formal training from René Princeteau and John Lewis Brown and then, after moving to Paris in 1881, he spent three years in Bonnat's atelier and a further year in Cormon's. He there acquired the Salon techniques, but was fascinated by Impressionism and Japonism, and was devoted to the works of Degas. The last ten years of his life were a great ferment, as he found and developed his style, concentrating on the life of the cabarets, nightclubs, and bordellos. His colour posters, executed directly on the lithographic stones, were of an extraordinarily controlled freedom, pushing the limits of Art Nouveau conventions to the extent of recreating them. He travelled to Brussels to meet van de Velde and to London to meet Oscar Wilde and Beardsley before dying at the age of thirty-seven.

Art Nouveau developed simultaneously in Belgium. This small country, at the crossroads between its great neighbours France and Germany, split between a French-speaking population which tended to look to France for its culture and a Flemish-speaking population with strong ties to the Netherlands, found itself in a great ferment in the 1880s, when various writers and artists grouped themselves under the slogan *'Soyons-Nous'* ('Let us be Ourselves'). The *Cercle des XX* (Group of the Twenty) was formed in 1884 by twenty artists who wished to organise exhibitions outside the confines of the official Salons. The group's Secretary was Octave Maus, who had earlier founded a magazine called *L'Art Moderne* in which to pursue the ideals of William Morris. In 1893 the group changed its name to *La Libre Esthétique*, opening its doors to the outside world. Many of the most advanced and creative artists from other countries were to exhibit in the *Libre Esthétique* annual Salons, which were also open to the crafts. Felicien Rops and his disciple Armand Rassenfosse were among the first Belgian artists to try their hands at producing modern posters, but it was not until the mid 1890s that the Belgian poster became one of the great manifestations of the Art Nouveau image.

Privat Livemont (1861-1936) was one of the finest practitioners. After studying at a School of Decorative Arts in Belgium, he spent six years in Paris, some under a study Scholarship he had been awarded, during which he both studied and worked on stage designs and architectural decorations. On his return to Belgium he concentrated on painting as well as teaching. He produced some thirty posters between

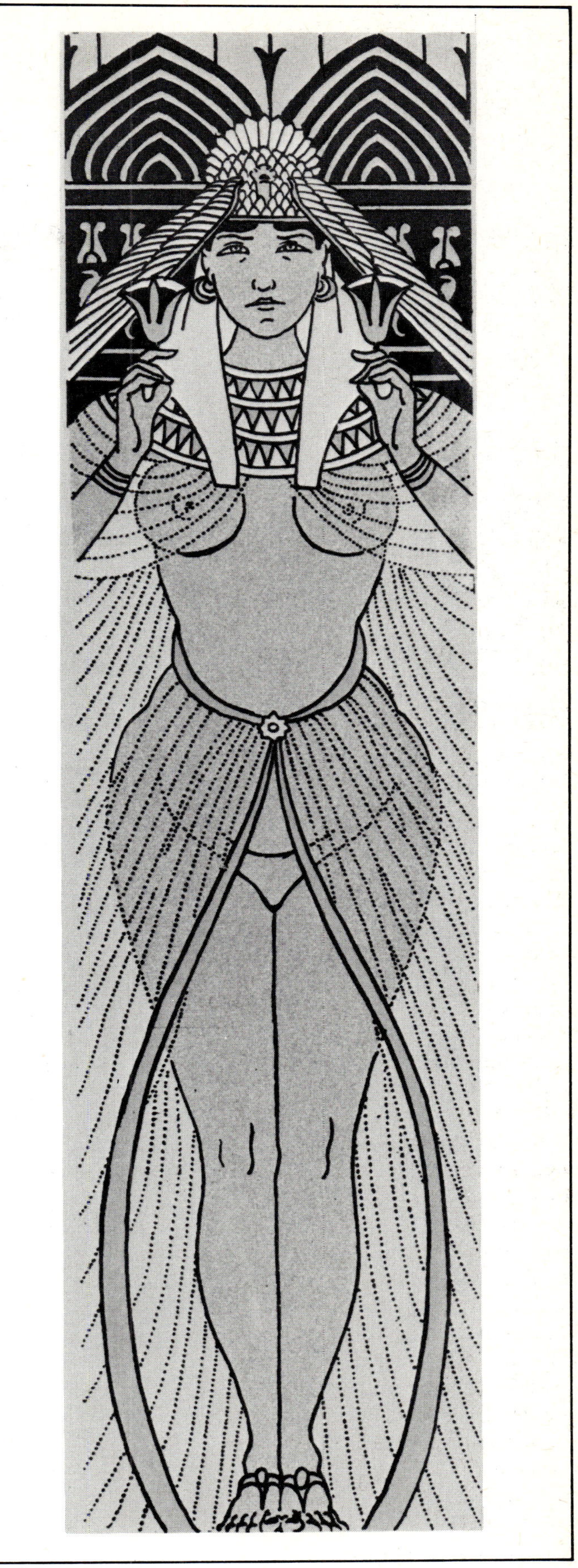

Alfred Roubille
*Princesse Orientale*

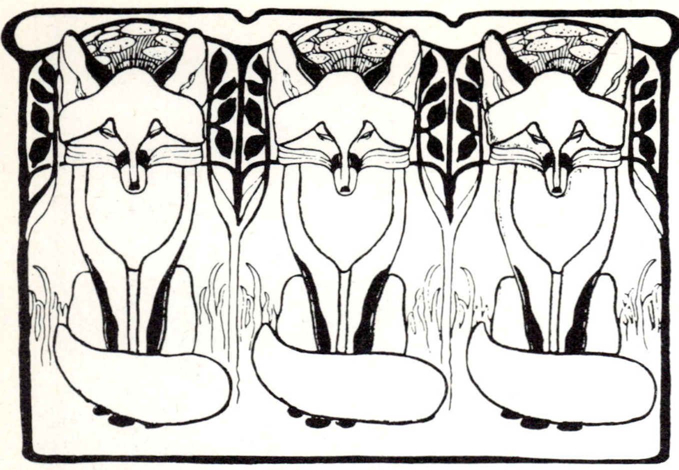

Ludwig Hohlwein
*Book decoration*

1890 and 1900, the majority executed after 1896, developing the theme of woman in an Art Nouveau manner. His women are languid, heavy-lidded, with strong profiles; the colours used are strong and flat; hair is treated as abstract tendrils. He developed a system of double outline, the strong black lines defining the silhouette being themselves outlined in white lines, giving a haloed cut-out effect against the coloured background. There is more than an echo of Mucha in Livemont's posters, yet their women are utterly unlike one another.

Henri Evenepoel (1872-1899) designed about a dozen posters, but did not live to execute many of them. After studying in Brussels he entered Gustave Moreau's atelier in Paris in 1892. In the few years before his death from typhus at the age of twenty-seven he produced paintings, watercolours and graphics, including a set of illustrations for Edgar Allen Poe, in a strongly personal style based on great simplification of line and colour.

Gisbert Combaz (1869-1941) only began to study art after giving up his law practice. A great collector of Far Eastern art and artifacts, he wrote several books on the subject, as well as becoming a professor of Fine Arts at various Belgian Institutes. He designed many of the posters for the *Libre Esthétique* annual Salons from 1895 onwards, exhibiting there himself many times after 1897. His poster for the 1899 Salon, perhaps the most dramatic one of all, is illustrated here, tree and thistle leaves, sun and sea conventionalised into decorative arabesques opposing areas of flat colour to create dynamic tension.

Henry van de Velde (1863-1957), architect, interior and industrial designer and painter, only produced one poster. This was for *Tropon*, a concentrated food, and dates from 1898, when the artist was put in charge of both advertising and graphic design of the product. A student of Carolus-Duran, van de Velde had been on the fringes of both Impressionist and Symbolist movements before joining the *Cercle des XX* in Brussels. The influence of William Morris and the example of English Arts and Crafts led to his turning to decoration and the applied arts. Van de Velde illustrated books, designed bookbindings, metalware, jewellery, and embroidery. In 1896 he designed four rooms for Bing's gallery, *L'Art Nouveau,* then, in 1899, he designed Meier-Graefe's new gallery, *La Maison Moderne.* He was one of the founders of the Deutsche Werkbund, and taught at the Weimar School of Applied Art, from which he was dismissed as an enemy alien at the outbreak of war in 1914, being succeeded there by Walter Gropius, who re-formed the School as the Bauhaus. Van de Velde's form of Art Nouveau is entirely abstract and ornamental, repeating motifs with minor variations to produce a tension which is yet totally two-dimensional.

Henry van de Velde
*Illustration*

German Art Nouveau, usually referred to as Jugendstil after the title of the magazine which helped to popularize it, *Jugend*, encompassed a wide variety of styles. The work of artists like Hans Christiansen (1866-1945), who studied at the *Académie* Julien in Paris and travelled widely, bore a strong resemblance to French and Belgian Art Nouveau. Thomas Theodor Heine (1867-1948), and Markus Behmer (1879-1958), developed an almost caricatural individuality based on a supple, expressive line with contrasting masses of black and white which was clearly inspired by Beardsley. Yet Beardsley's style found its most individual and quirky adept in another German artist, Hans Henning, Baron Voight (1887-1969), who drew under the pseudonym Alastair. Born in Karlsruhe, Alastair was a composer, musician and dancer, a selt-taught artist and fashion designer. His first illustrated books date from 1908, his decadent, evil characters dancing elegantly through a series of French, English, American and German publications. The Munich Seccession comprised many Art Nouveau illustrators, including Peter Behrens, August Endell, Otto Ekmann and Bruno Paul. Hans Höppener (1868-1948), who drew under the name Fidus, worked within a basically Symbolist framework, developing a mystical theosophy through the creation of a curious ideal city peopled with worshipping nudes. He illustrated many books.

In the Netherlands Jan Toorop (1858-1928), born in Java but educated in Amsterdam, also studied in Brussels where he joined the *Groupe des XX.* He was soon involved in the Symbolist movement, and later exhibited with the Rose+Croix in Paris. His style was a curious mixture of strong, undulating lines writhing continuously to fill the entire surface with pattern, interpreting his mystical subjects as Javanese stick puppets with elongated, boneless limbs thrown into expressive gestures with equally boneless bodies floating their way into the pattern of the whole. His most successful poster was

*Delftsche Slaolie* (1895), a salad oil, in which the hair of the two figures forms renewing patterns filling up the whole of the available surface. His use of colour was surprisingly discreet, *Delftsche Slaolie* being in muted purple and yellow. Other posters frequently tend to the monochrome, *Arbeid Voor de Vrau*, for instance, being entirely maroon on white. Toorop's drawing, *The Three Brides* (1893), was reproduced in the September 1893 issue of *The Studio*.

The inaugural issue of *The Studio* in April had reproduced a series of drawings by Aubrey Beardsley, and the conjunction of these two artists, Beardsley and Toorop, was to have an enormous influence on four young Scottish students who were later to meet at the Glasgow School of Art, Charles Rennie Mackintosh (1868-1928), J. Herbert McNair (1868-1955), and Margaret Macdonald (1865-1933), who was to marry Mackintosh in 1900, and her younger sister Frances (1874-1921), who was to marry McNair in 1899. Later to be known as The Four, these young artists collaborated on a number of projects. The men were architects, and Mackintosh was to prove one of the most original and creative designers whenever given the opportunity. Through him the rectilinear entered Art Nouveau design, his patterns elongating and simplifying the human form to the extent of transforming it into a decorative motif. The Macdonald sisters were imbued with Symbolist ideals formed through strong religious conviction: their work communicated an artistic mysticism. Margaret Macdonald, in particular, greatly influenced Mackintosh in his development of ornamentation, bringing her dream world of ecstatic forms to her husband's soaring lines. The Four's graphic output, though small, is outstanding. Some of it, particularly in the case of posters, was collaborative.

The four were at various times surrounded by friends and disciples. One of two important graphic artists was Jessie Marion King (1876-1949), who studied at the Glasgow School of Art between 1894 and 1900 before teaching bookbinding there. Married to A.E. Taylor, she designed fabrics and painted murals, but especially illustrated books in a medieval fairyland style with a deliberately shaky fine line. The other was Annie French (1872-1965), who moved to London from Glasgow and also illustrated many books. Both these artists helped diffuse the Glasgow style, each interpreting it in an intensely personal way.

The Four were invited to exhibit in the 1896 Arts and Crafts Exhibition in London. They showed a number of posters, a watercolour, some beaten metal ware by the Macdonald sisters and a Mackintosh settle. The organisers were disturbed and displeased, and did not invite them again. Gleeson White, editor of *The Studio* was, however, sufficiently impressed to visit them, see more of their work and write two articles published in his magazine in 1897 under the title

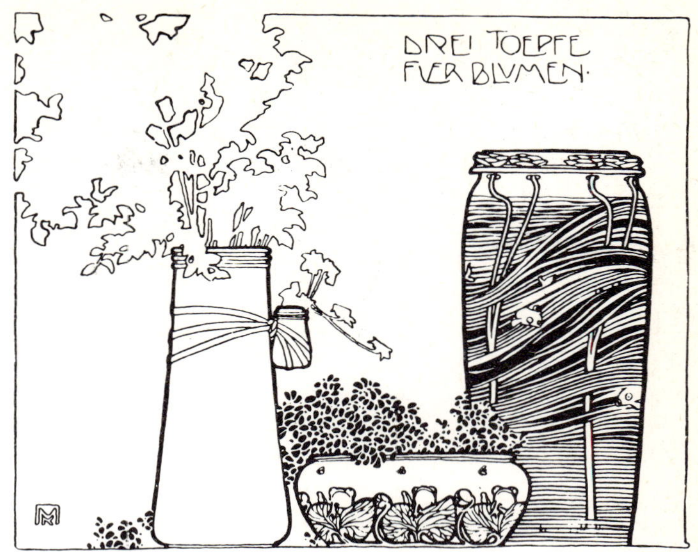


Kolo Moser
*Illustration*

'Some Glasgow Designers and Their Work'. *The Studio* was widely read in Europe, and these articles led to a further one written by Alexander Koch in the German review *Dekorative Kunst* in 1898. From that time onwards Mackintosh and his group were more admired and appreciated in Germany and in Austria than at home.

Austrian Art Nouveau itself was strongly influenced by Mackintosh. Artists attracted by this style, which was now being thought of as an *international* style, grouped themselves around Gustav Klimt (1862-1918) and Joseph Hoffman (1870-1955) to found the Vienna *Secession* in 1897. A year later they launched a new magazine, *Ver Sacrum,* as their official publication to popularize both Austrian and foreign artists. Though late starters in Art Nouveau, the Vienna artists soon developed a characteristic Secession style which, particularly in the crafts, was transitional between high Art Nouveau and Art Deco.

Franco-British artists were paramount in the creation of American Art Nouveau. Grasset designed magazine covers for *Frank Leslie's Illustrated Newspaper* in 1882 and for *Harper's Bazaar* in 1889, 1891 and 1892. He also produced two posters for the *Century Magazine's* serialization of an illustrated "Life of Napoleon" in 1893. Another French artist, Luc Metivet, won a competition to design a further Napoleonic poster for the *Century*.

The two artists primarily responsible for the development of the Art Nouveau image in the United States were Louis Rhead and Will Bradley. Rhead (1857-1926) was, in fact, born in England. Educated at the South Kensington Art School and in Paris, he emigrated to the United States in 1883 where, after working as an illustrator, he designed his first poster in 1890. He returned to Europe the following year, and spent the next three years between Paris and London. In the former city he became a disciple of Grasset's. On his return to the States he concentrated on the production of posters and magazine illustrations, and held a one-man exhibition in New York in 1895 and at the Salon des Cent in Paris in 1897.

William H. Bradley (1868-1962), born in Boston, was a self-taught artist working in Chicago. He immersed himself in the works of William Morris, but was most strikingly influenced by Aubrey Beardsley's fine, serpentine line, which led him to an almost abstract decorative whirl which was intricate, involved, and highly effective. He designed a number of posters, books, magazines and brochures and published his own magazine, *Bradley: His Book.* Around the two artists a number of other highly talented designers worked within the Art Nouveau convention, including Edward Penfield (1866-1925), who derived his images from those of the Swiss artist Steinlen and Toulouse-Lautrec; others included Will Carqueville, Frank Hazenplug, J.C. Leyendecker, Maxfield Parrish, Florence Lundborg and Ethel Reed.

The turn of the century saw the emergence of a new twist to the Art Nouveau image in Britain. William Nicholson (1872-1949) produced a series of magnificent woodcut portraits of notables, the most striking of which were those of Sarah Bernhardt and Whistler. Though simplified and stylised, these were not outlined patterns like those of Vallotton, but psychological portraiture treated rather like bleached out photographs. He used this technique to produce a variety of illustrated books on Sports, and London Types, and even an Alphabet. He also produced a number of posters in conjunction with his brother-in-law, James Pryde, under the pseudonym Beggarstaff Brothers. The most striking poster they produced was, unfortunately, never used. Designed for the Lyceum Theatre production of *Don Quixote*, the original is at the Victoria and Albert Museum in London, and was only issued in a small size for collectors by the *Maitre de L'Affiche* series in Paris.

The Art Nouveau image, diverse and perverse, flourished for only two decades, yet elements of it are still found in current pictorial art and advertising. The illustrations in this volume show the image at the height ot its glory.

All illustrations reproduced on the following pages are from colour lithograph posters and lithograph illustrations except for the following: Felix Vallotton, *La Paresse, Trois baigneuses, La belle épingle*; Wilhelm List, *Strahlenküsse*; Leopold Stolba, *Ver Sacrum: April*, all woodcuts; Tamagno, *La Moto-pompe Paul Noël*, watercolour design for a poster; Aubrey Beardsley, *The Black Cape, The Stomach Dance, The Toilet of Salomé*, all process engravings.

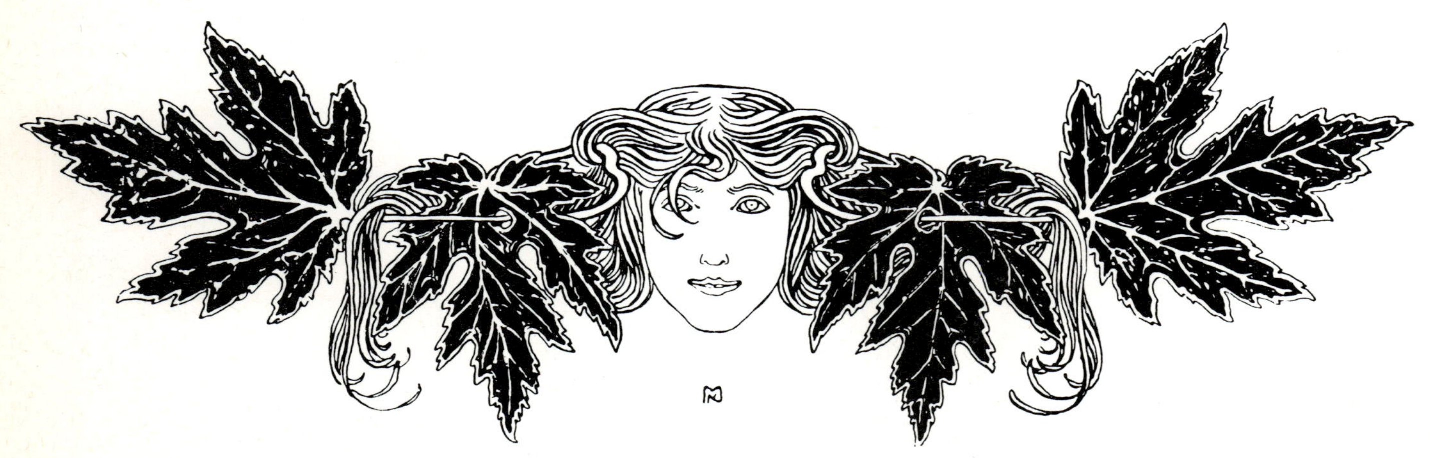

Kolo Moser
*Illustration*

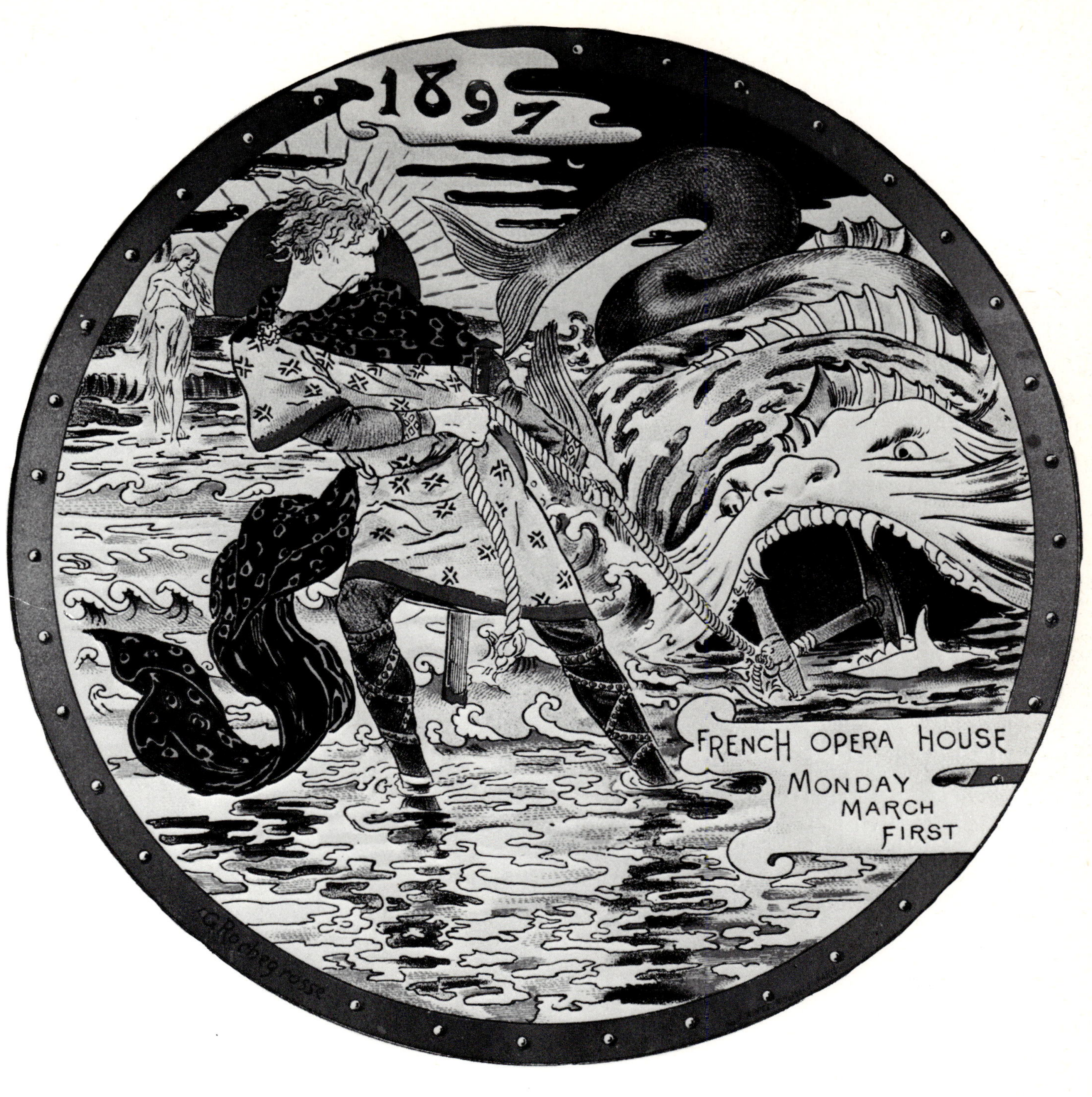


Georges Rochegrosse
*L'Opéra* 1897

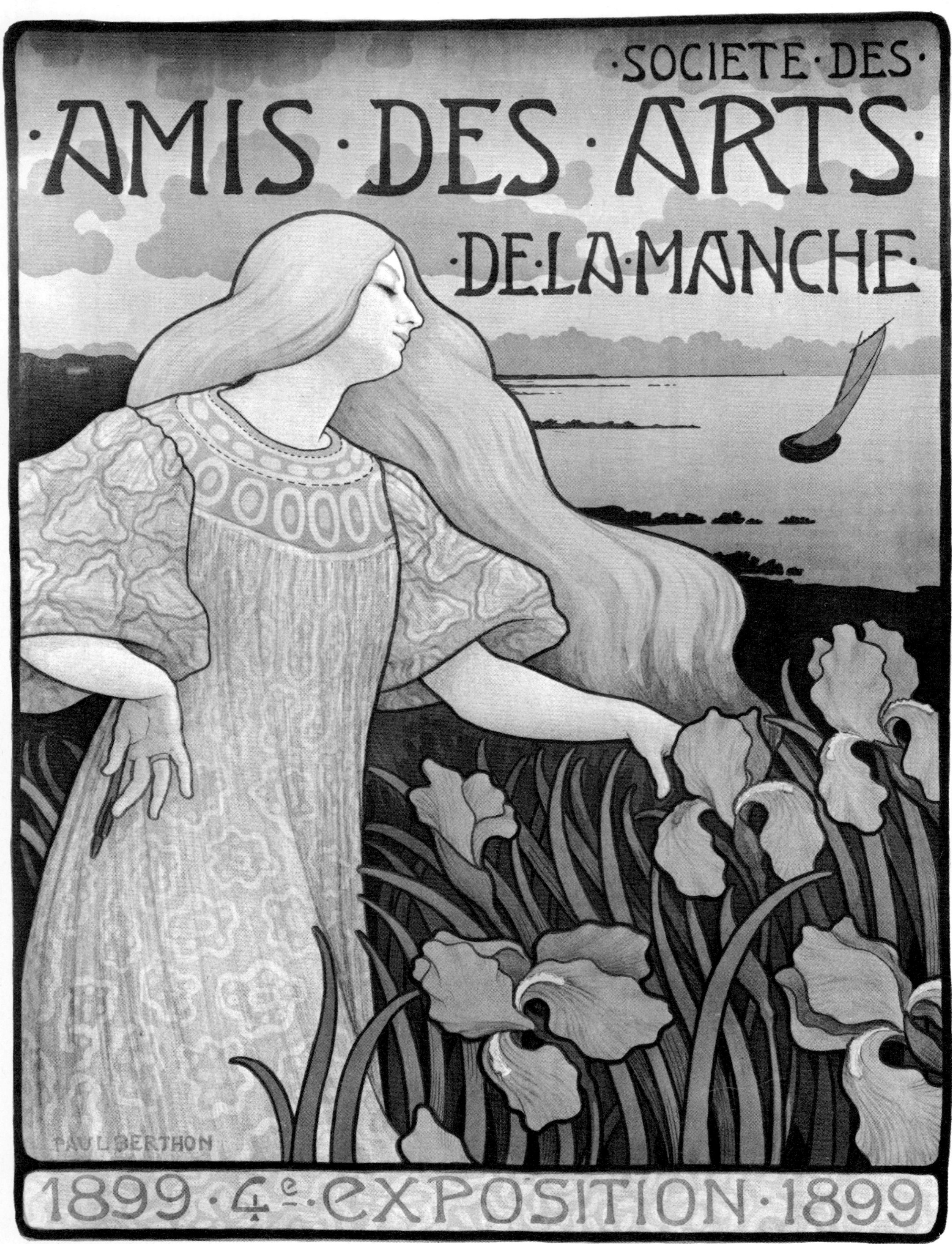


Paul Berthon
*Société des amis des arts de la Manche* 1899

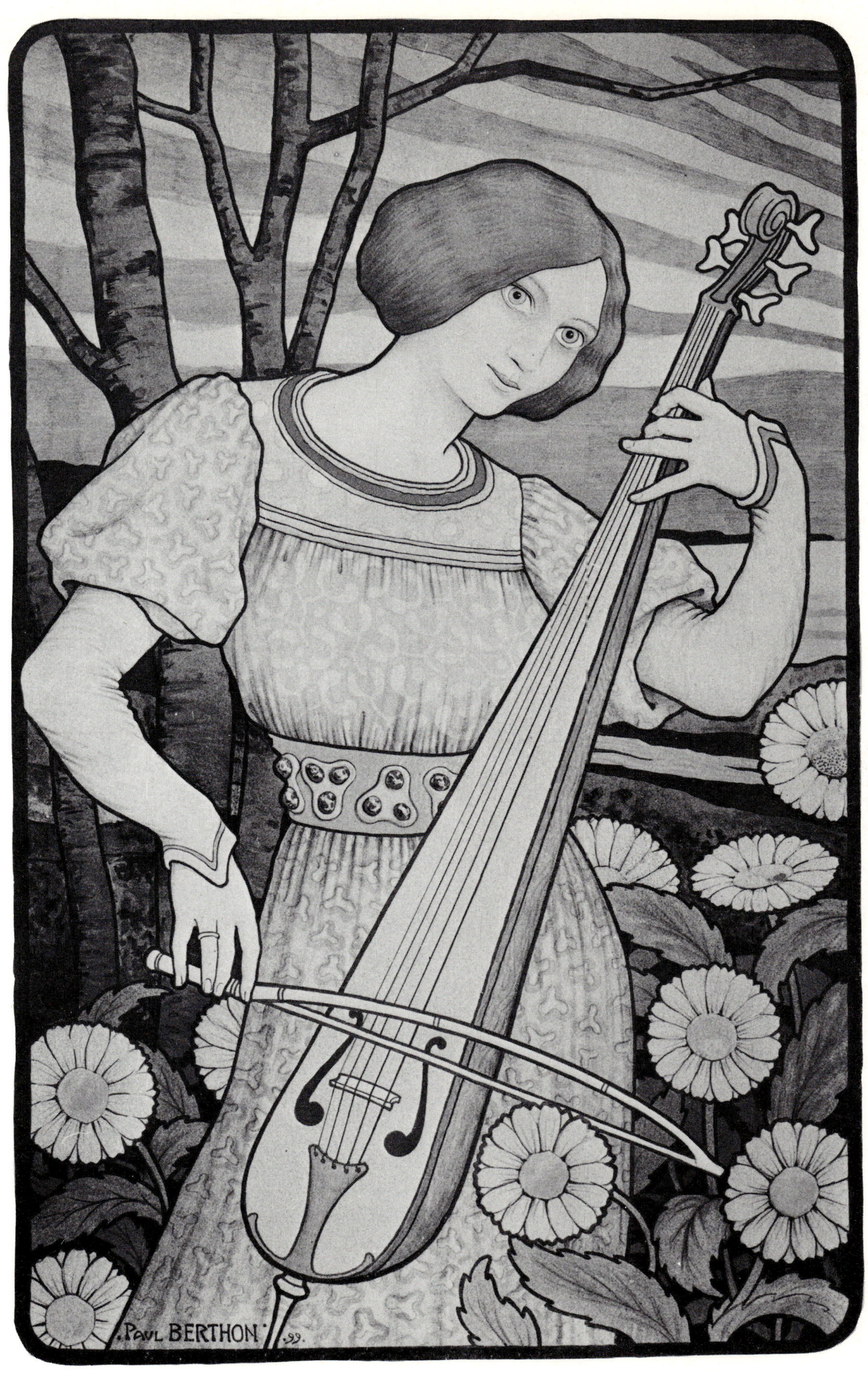


Paul Berthon
*La Viole de gambe* 1899

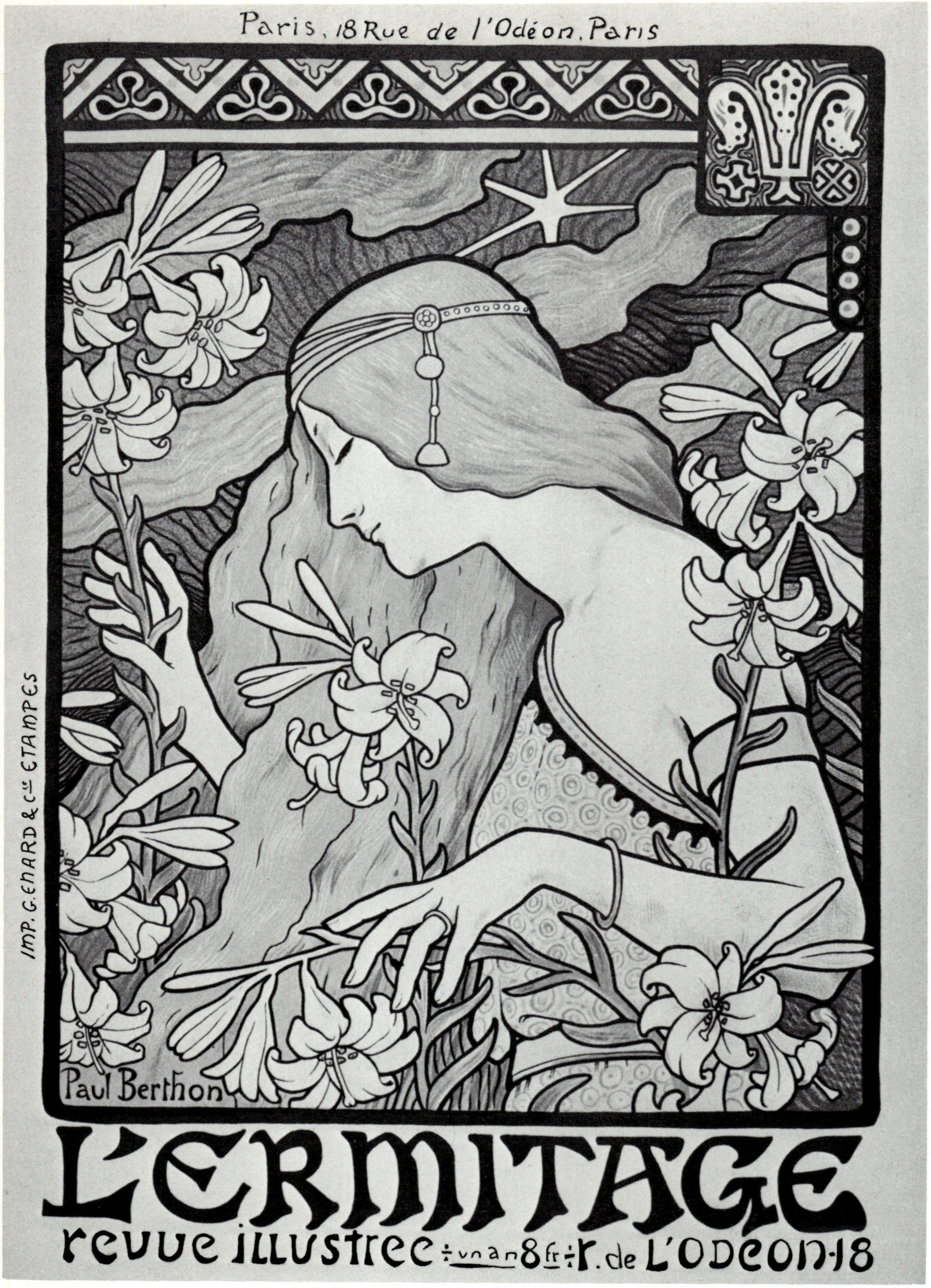

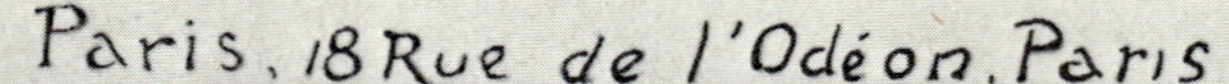


Paul Berthon
*L'Ermitage* 1900

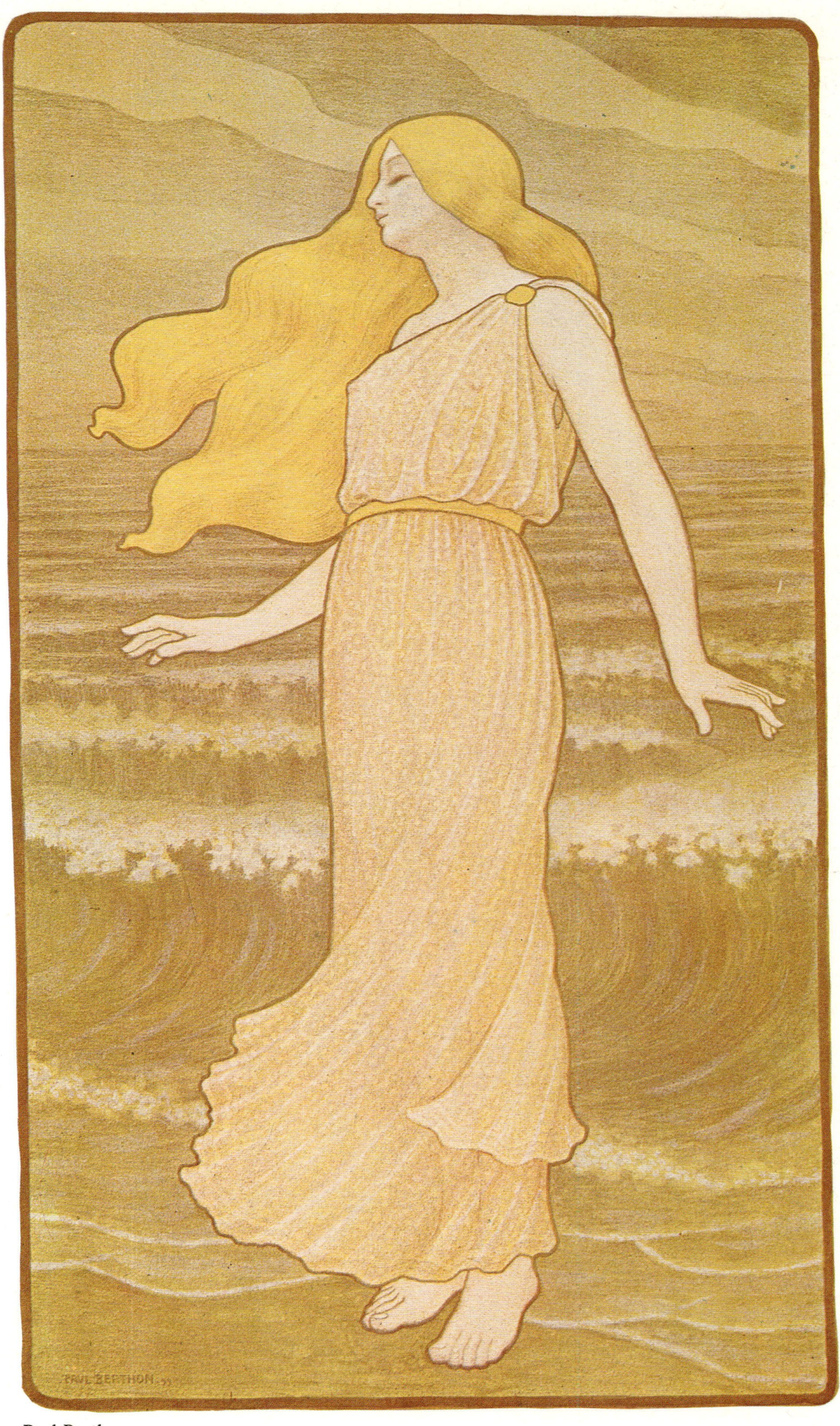


Paul Berthon
*La Vague* 1899

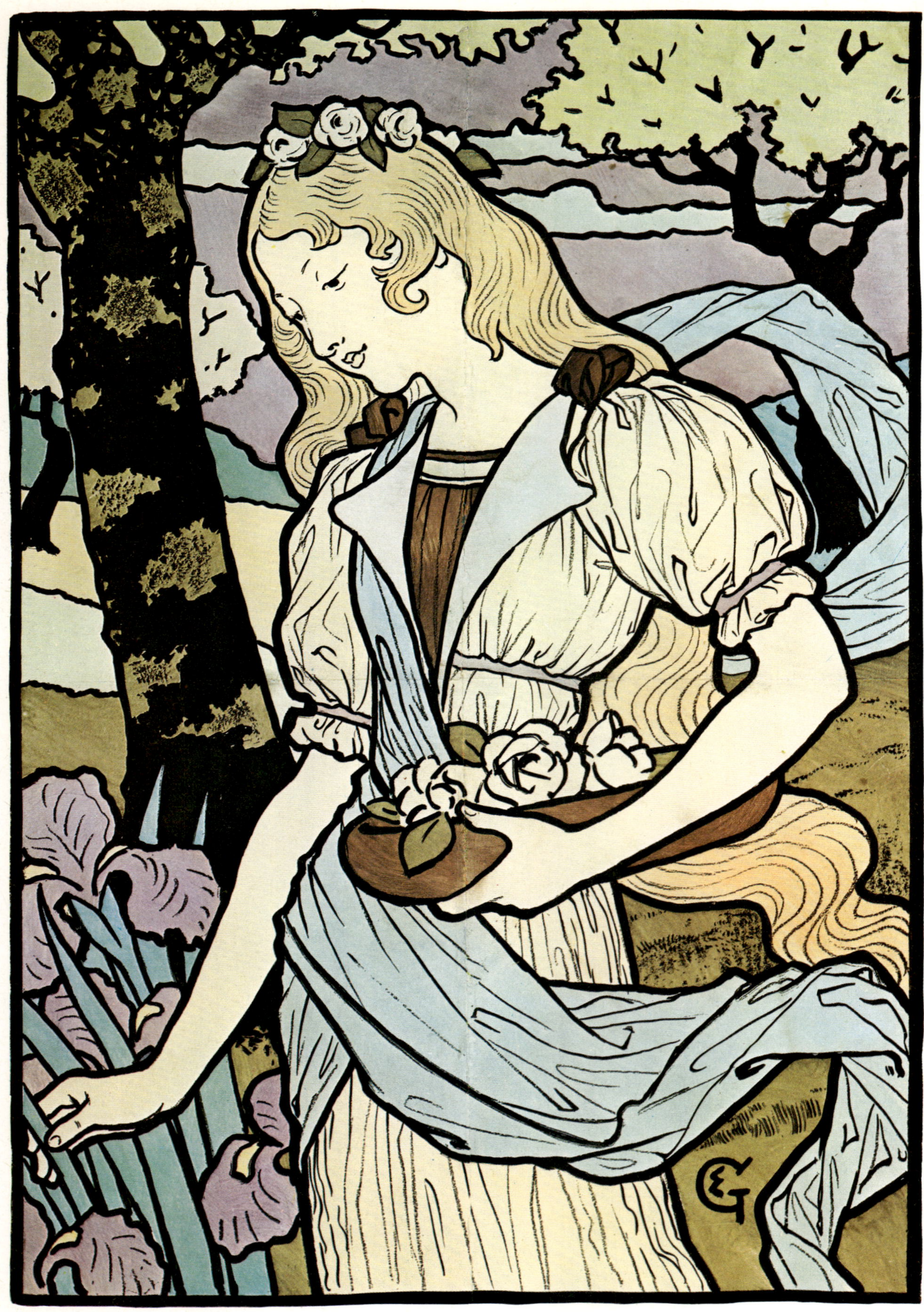

Eugène Grasset
*Grafton Gallery* 1893

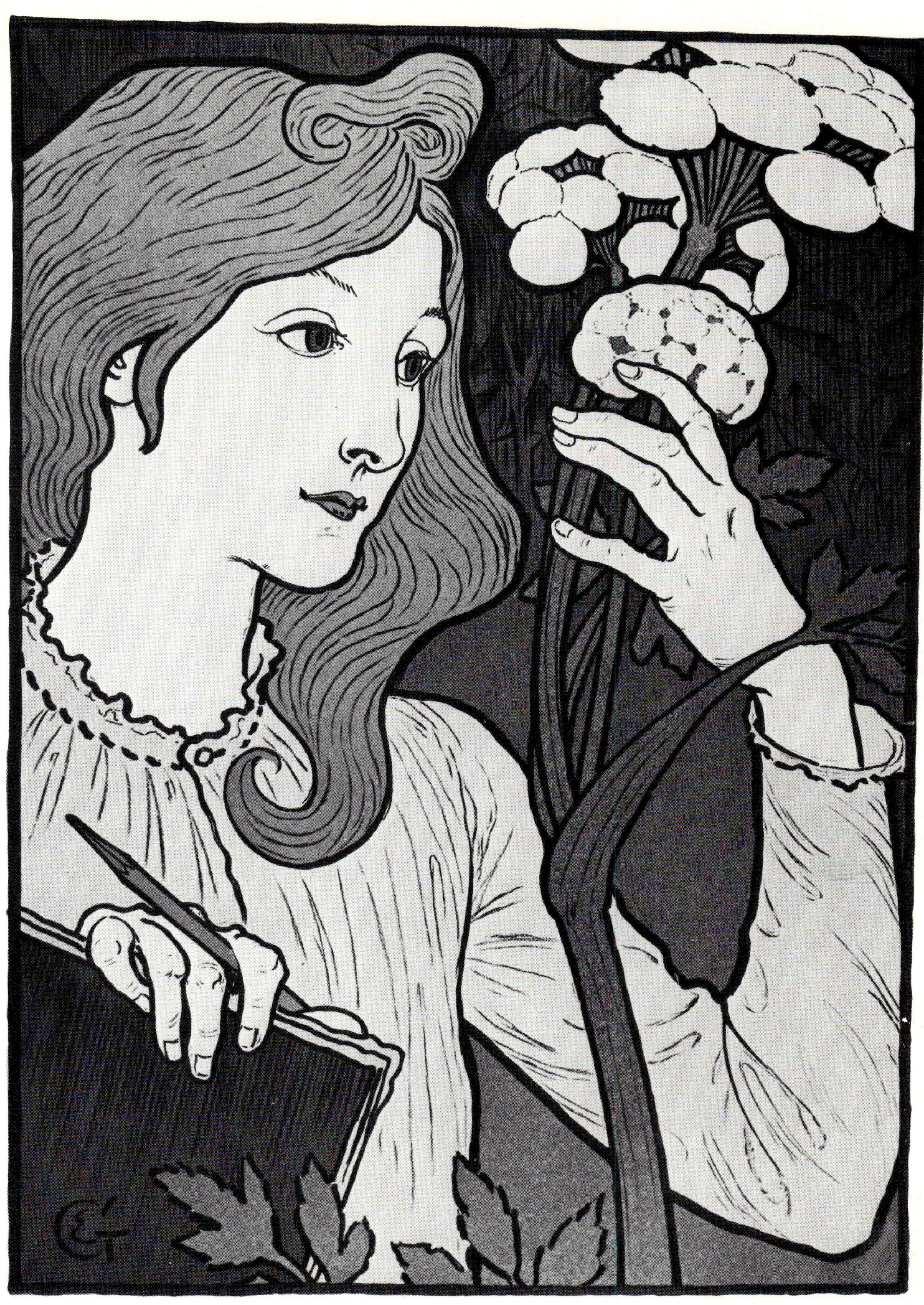

Eugène Grasset
*Salon des cent* (exposition Grasset) 1894

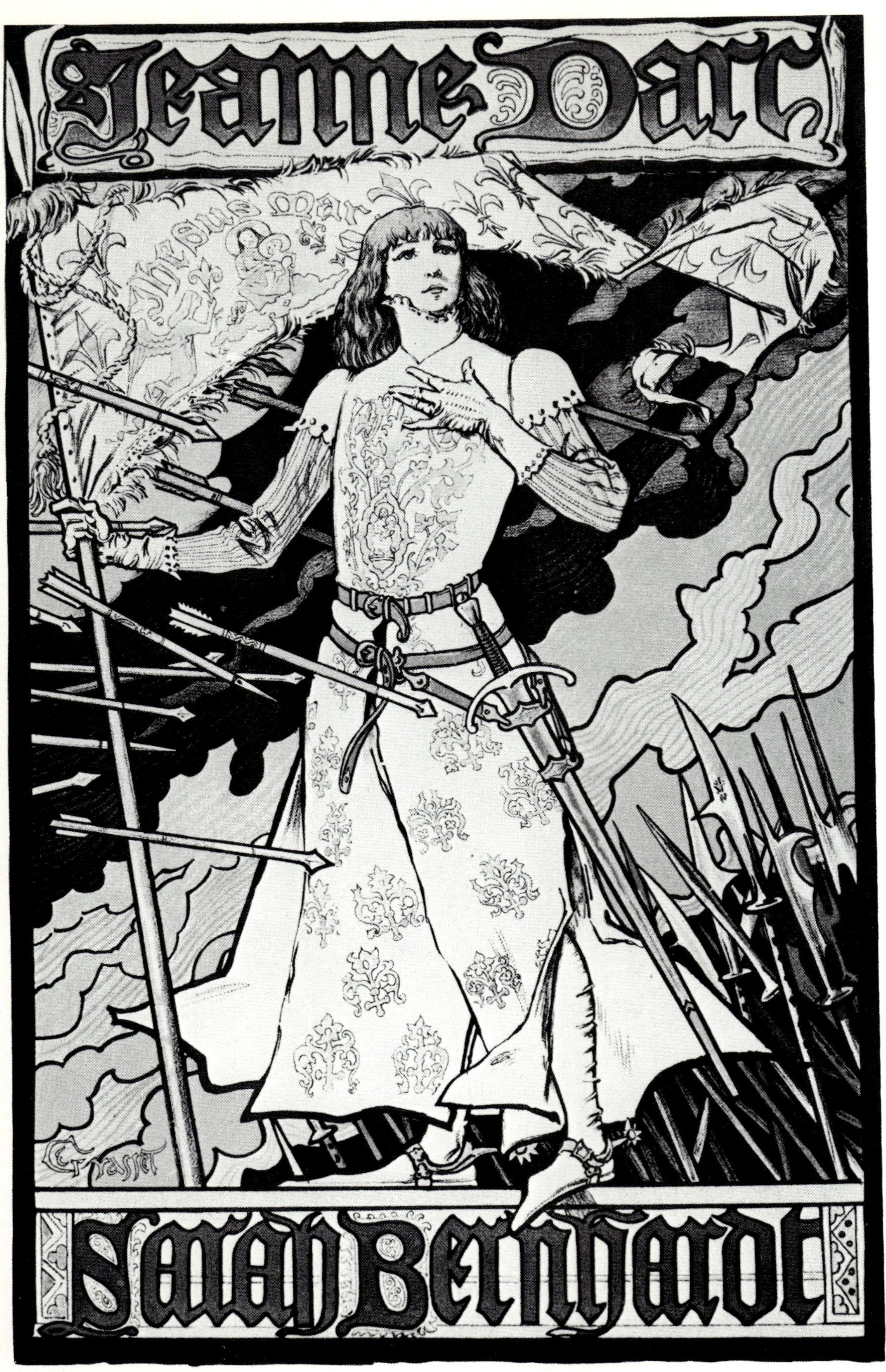


Eugène Grasset
*Sarah Bernhardt – Jeanne d'Arc* 1894

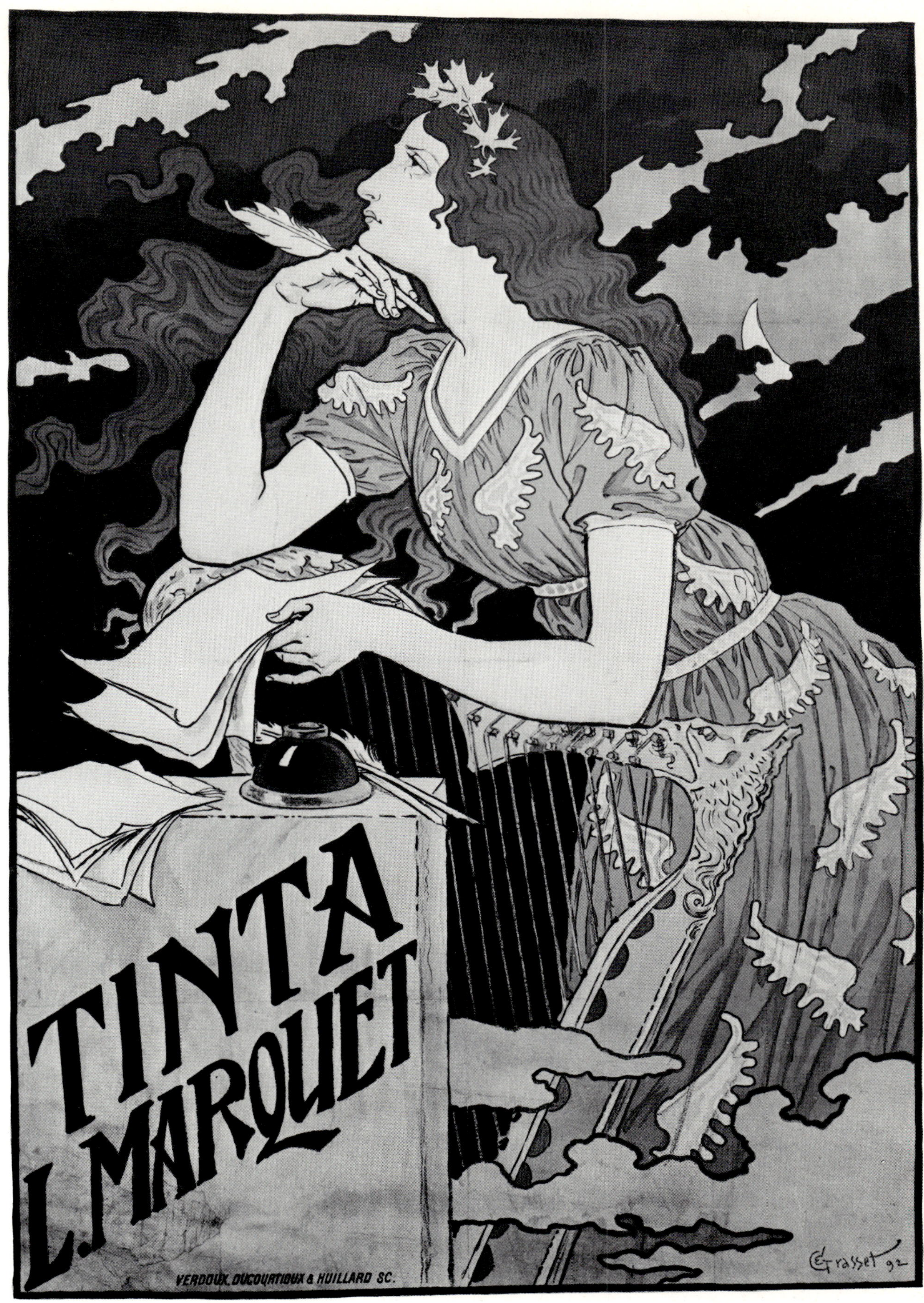

Eugène Grasset
*Tinta L. Marquet* 1892

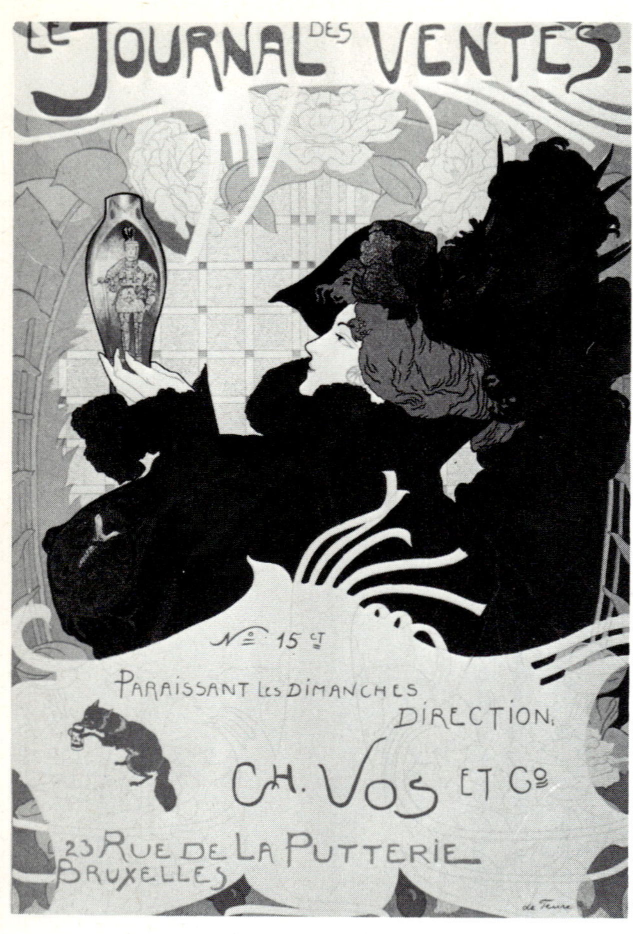


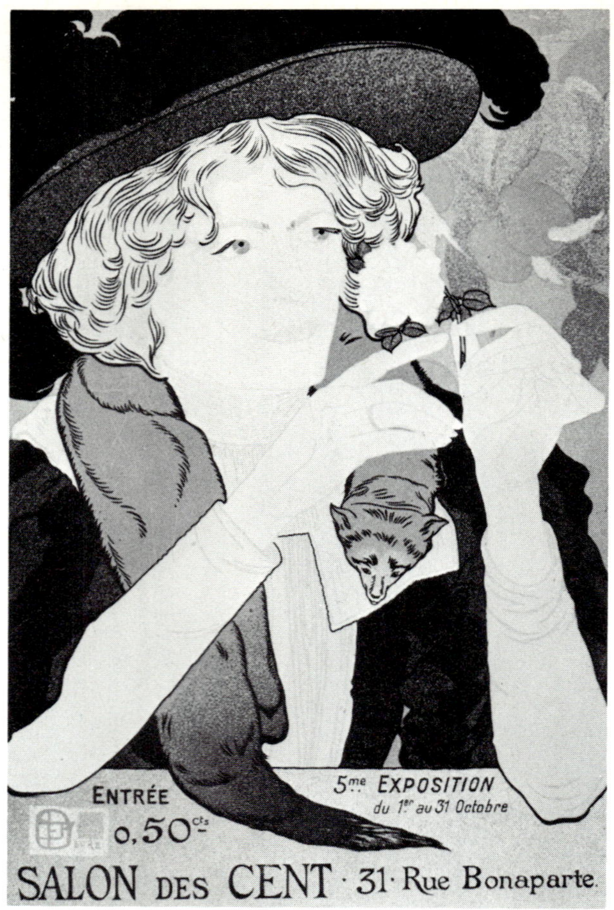


Georges de Feure
*Le Journal des ventes* 1898

Georges de Feure
*Salon des cent* 1896

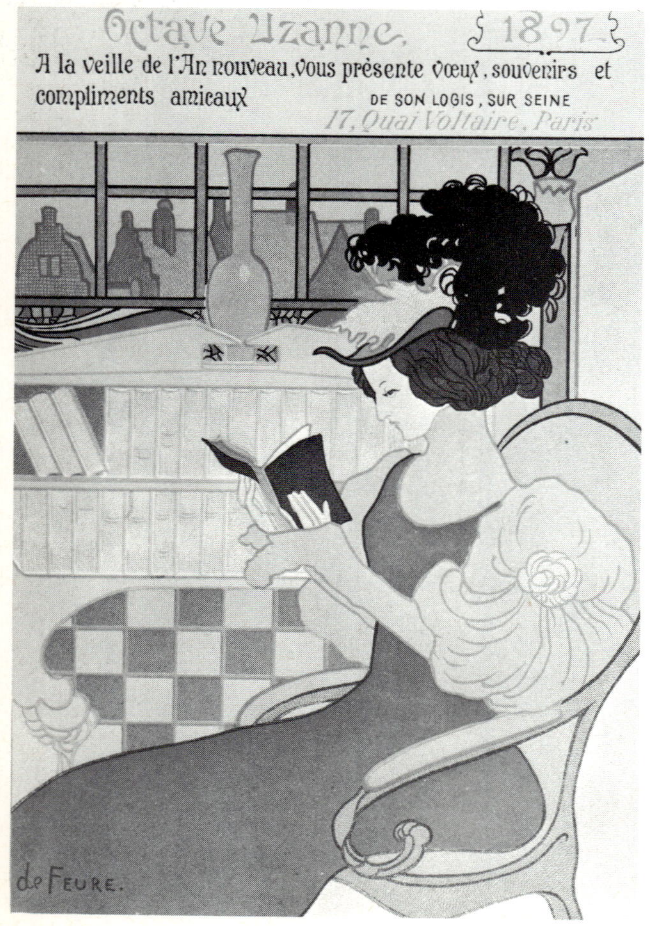


Georges de Feure
*Octave Uzanne* 1897

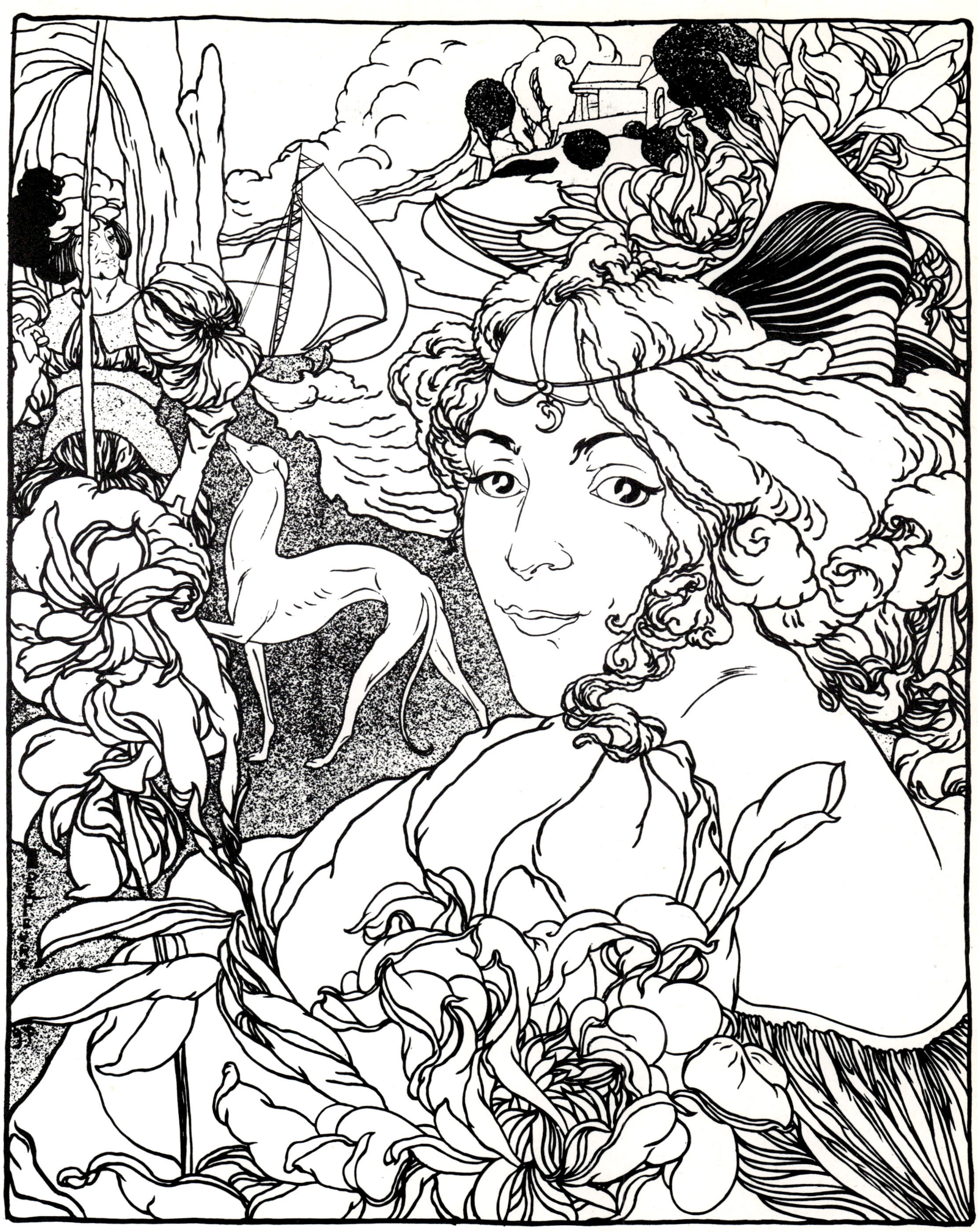

Georges de Feure
*Retour* 1897

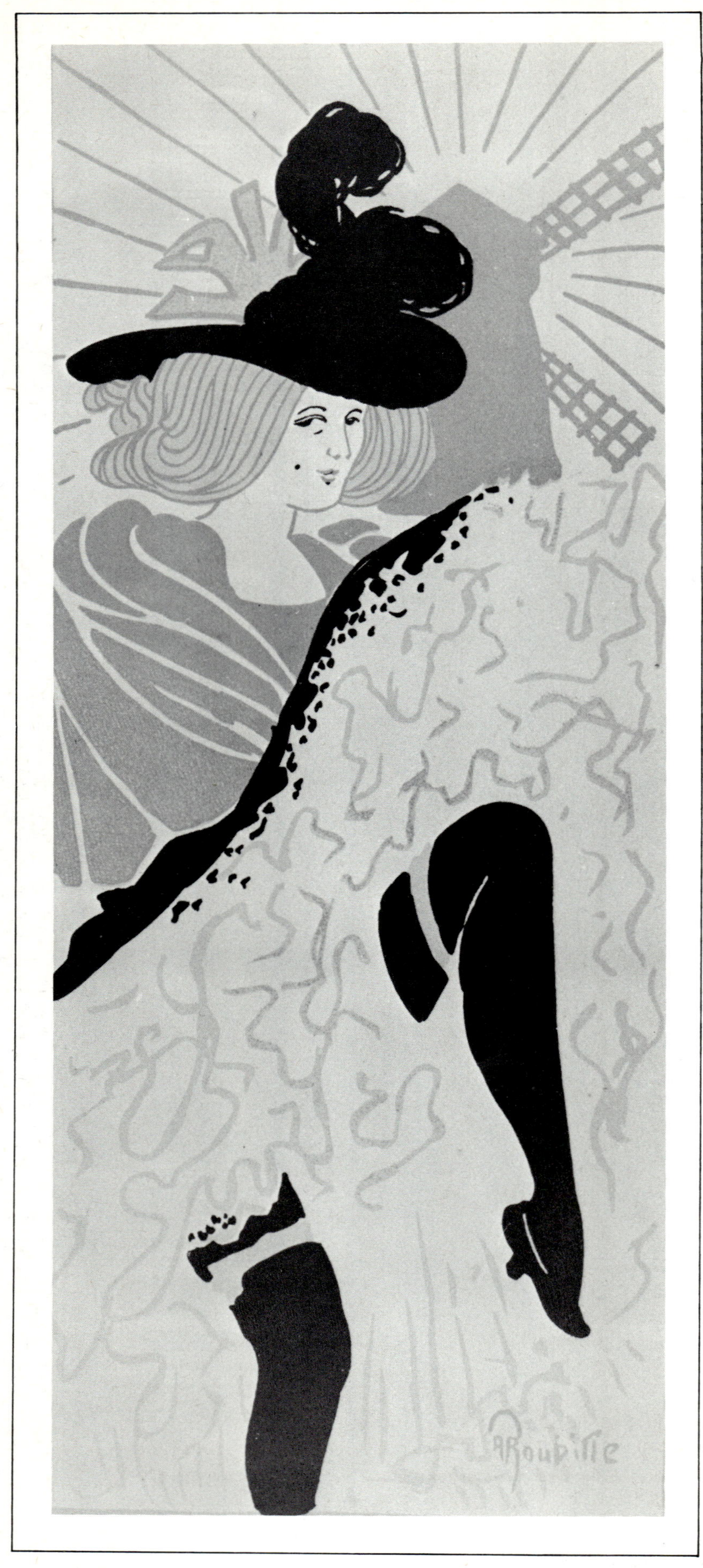


Alfred Roubille
*Moulin Rouge*

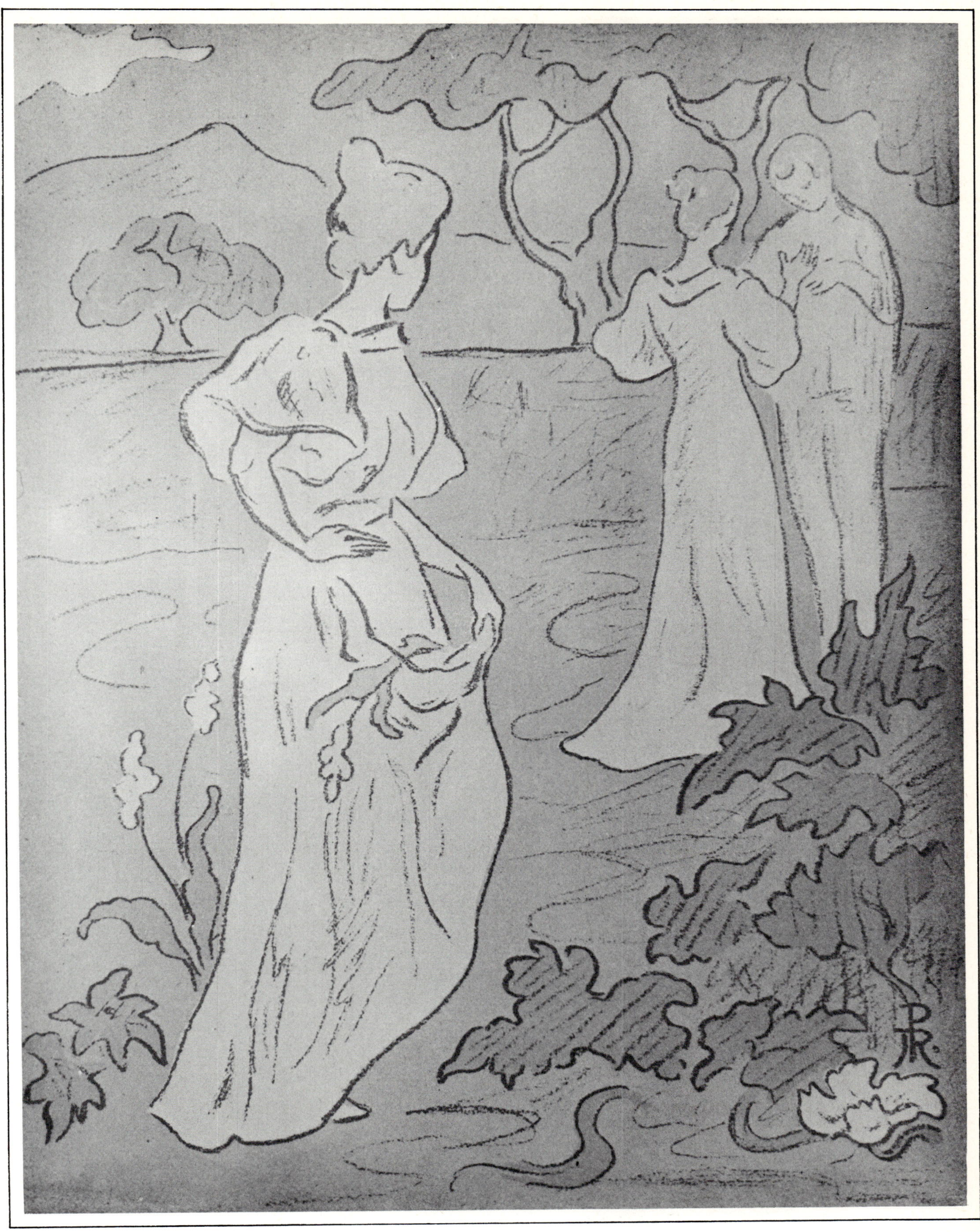

Paul Ranson
*Tristesse!* 1896

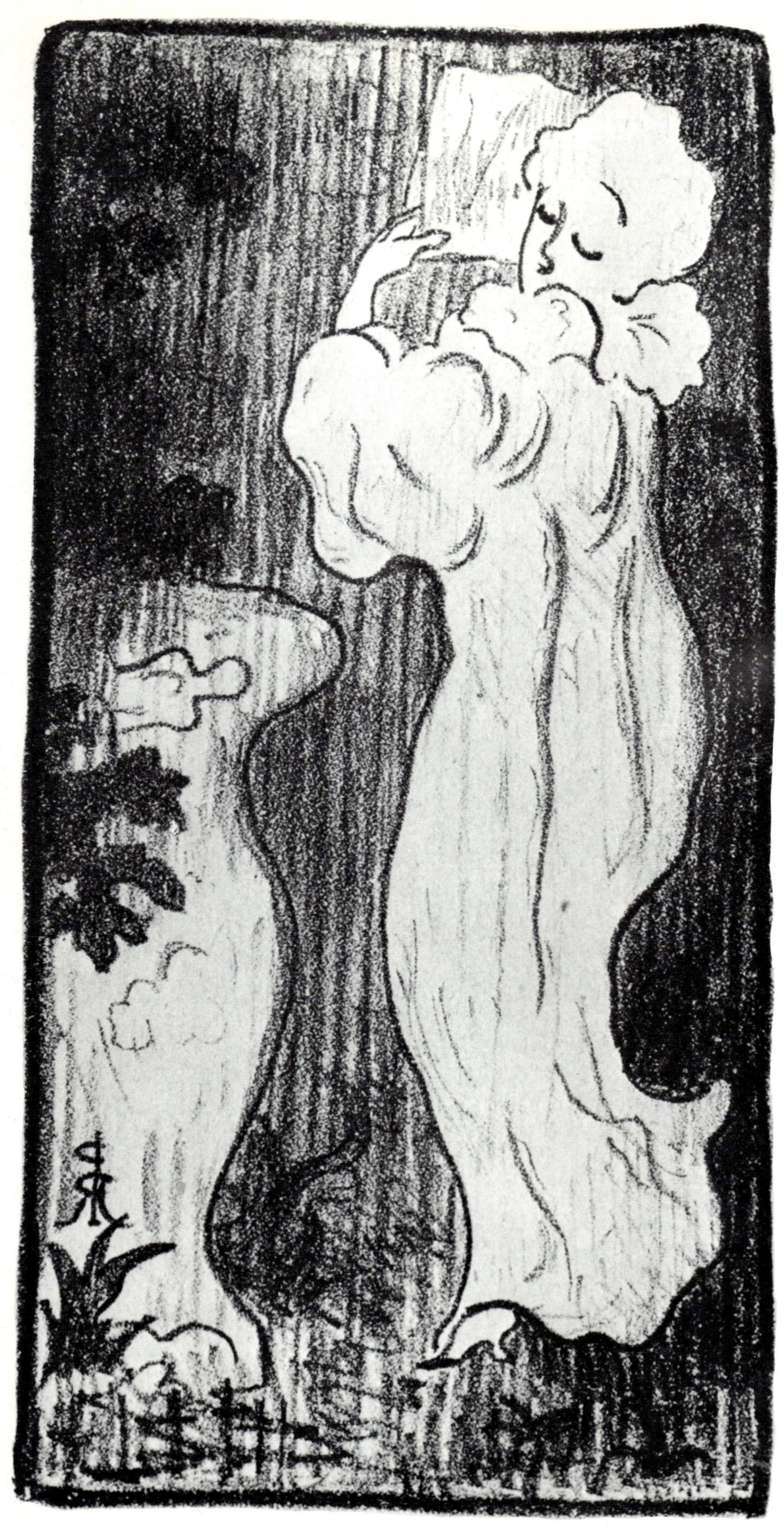

Paul Ranson
*La Revue blanche: La Liseuse* 1894

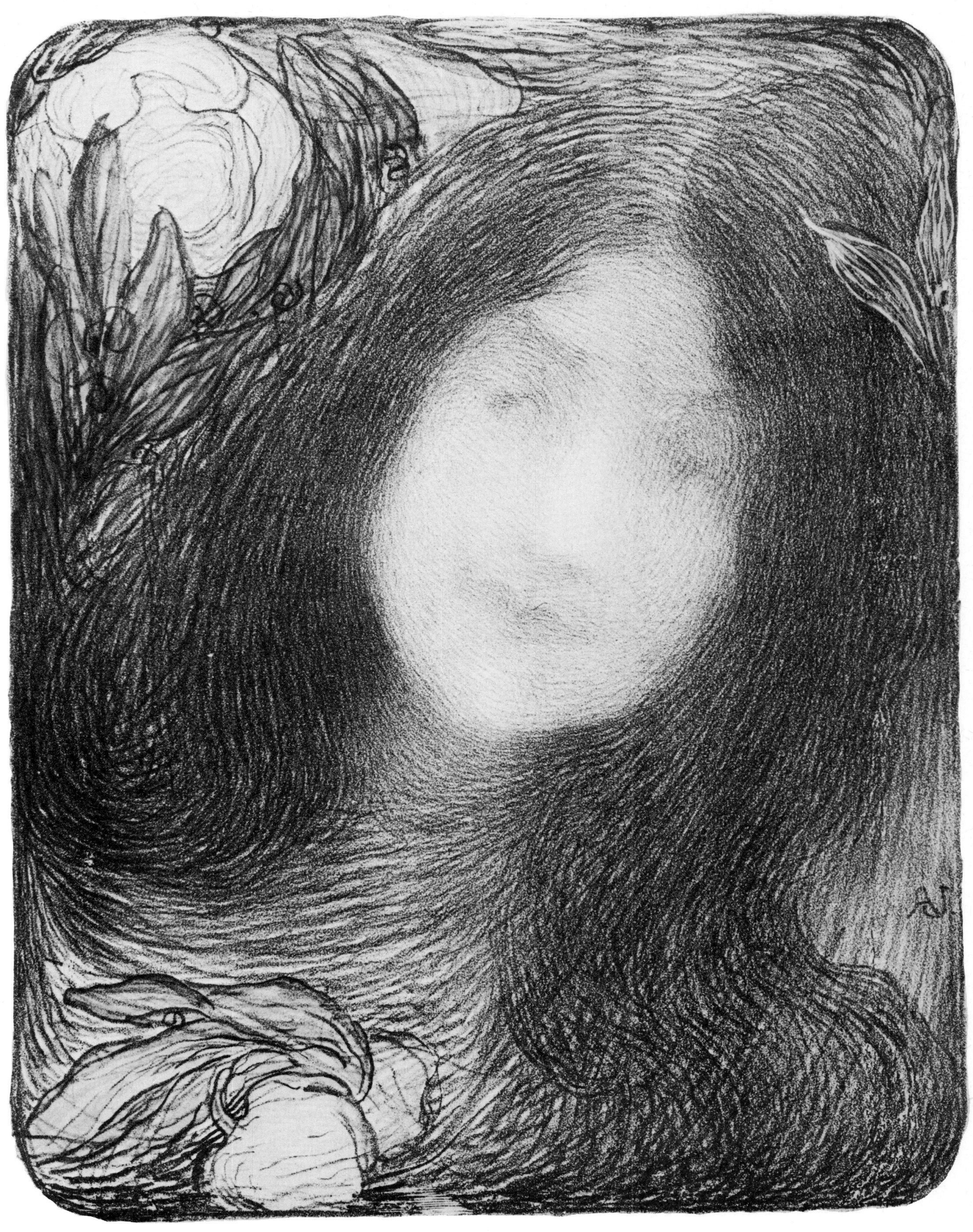

Edmond-François Aman-Jean
*Sous les fleurs*

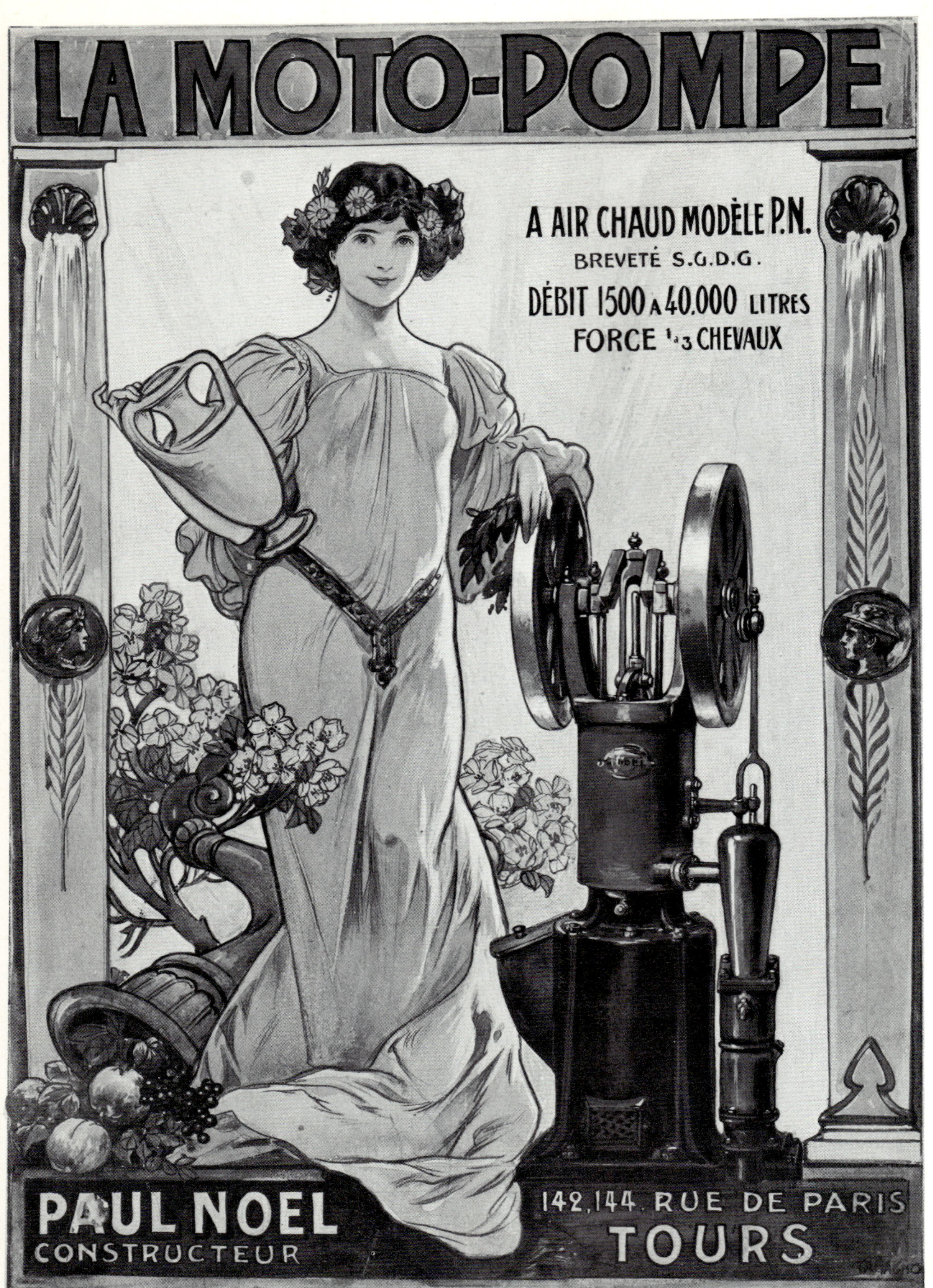


Tamagno
*La Moto-pompe Paul Noël*

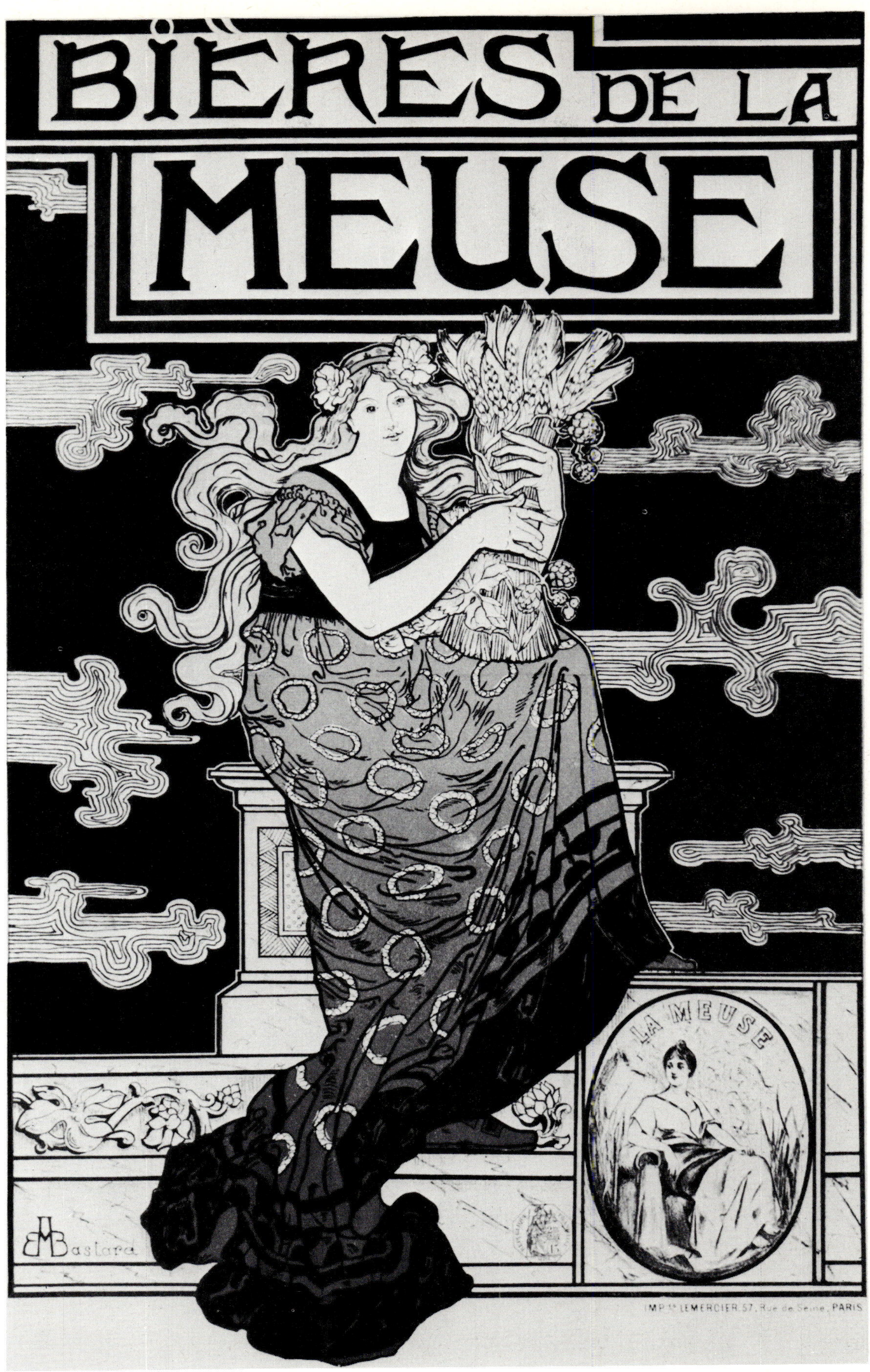


E.M. Bastard
*Bières de la Meuse*

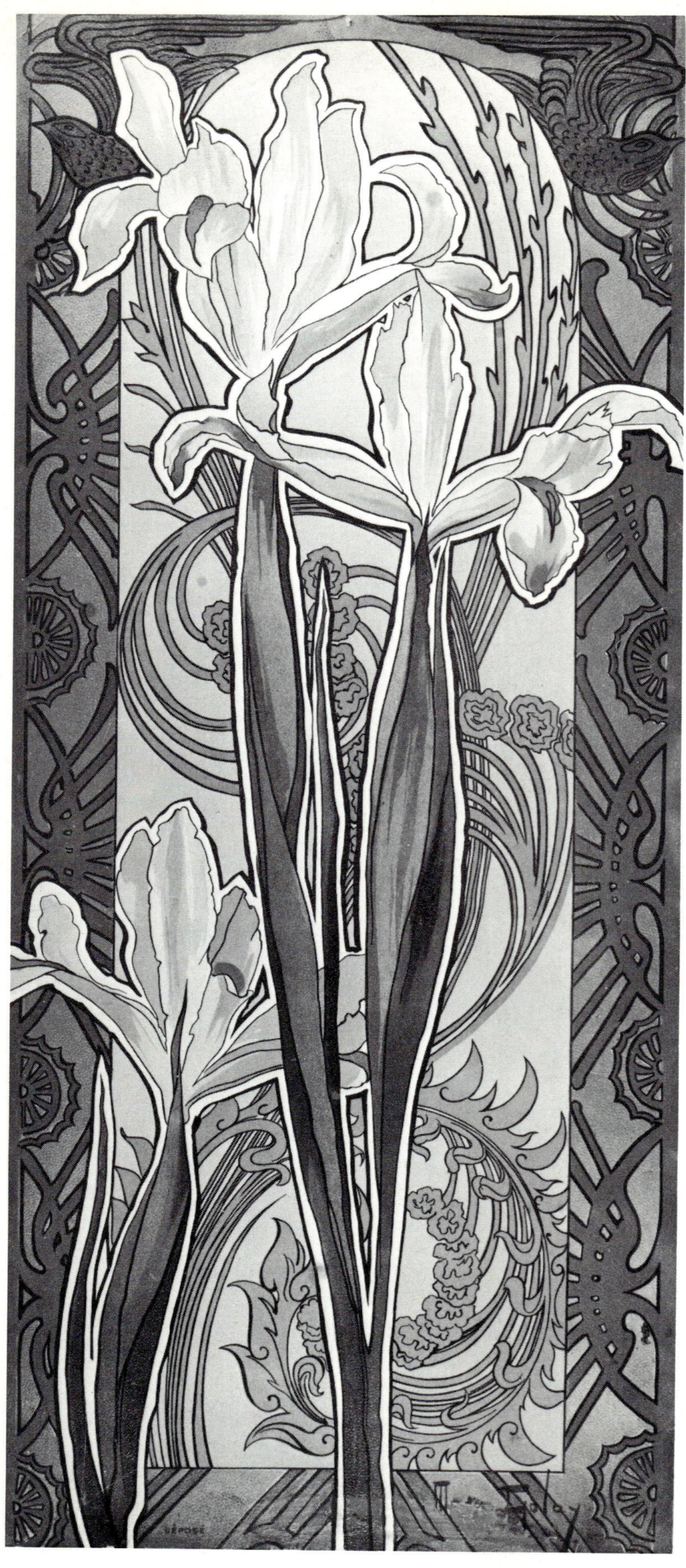

Mary Golay
*Iris blanc*

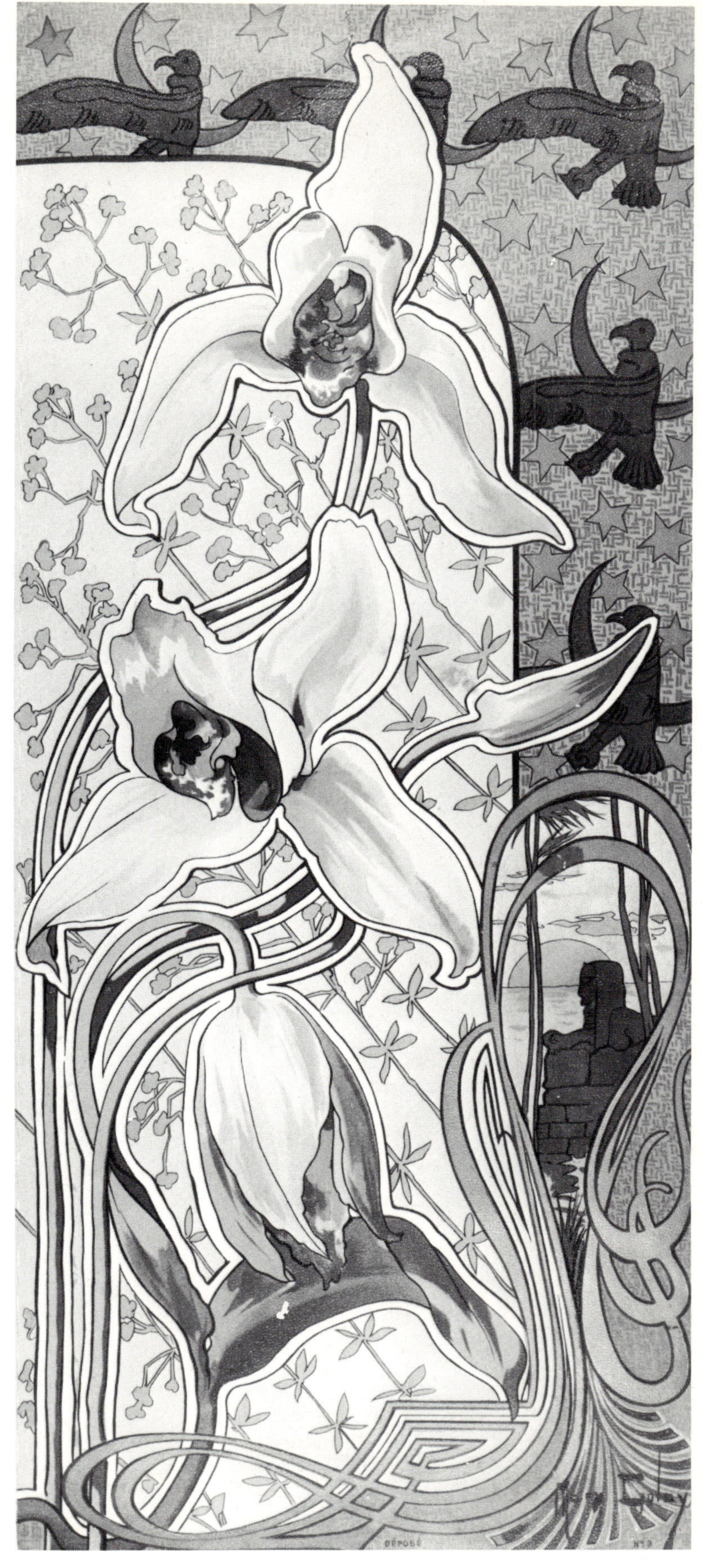

Mary Golay
*Orchidée*

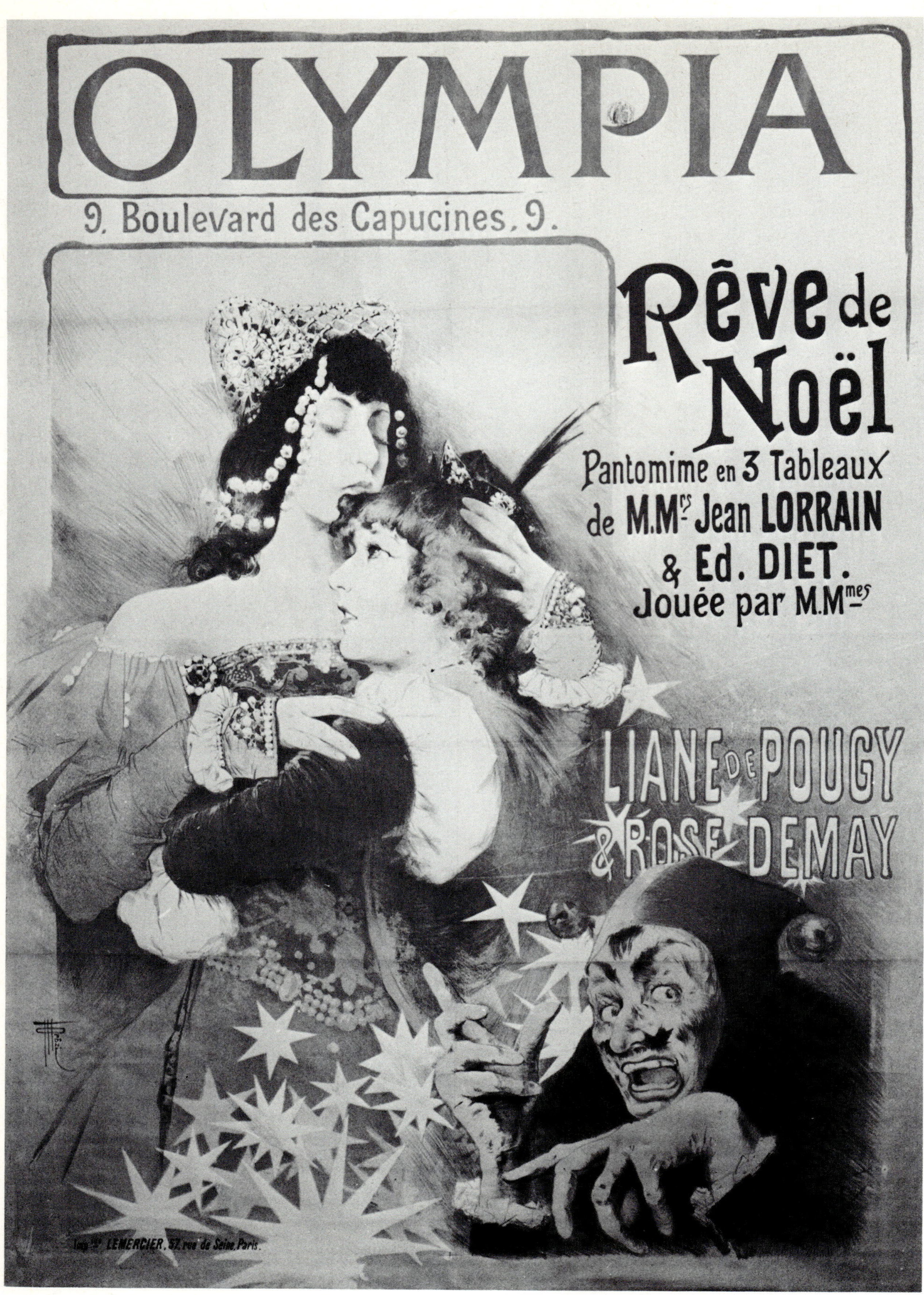


Manuel Orazi
*Olympia: Rêve de Noël*

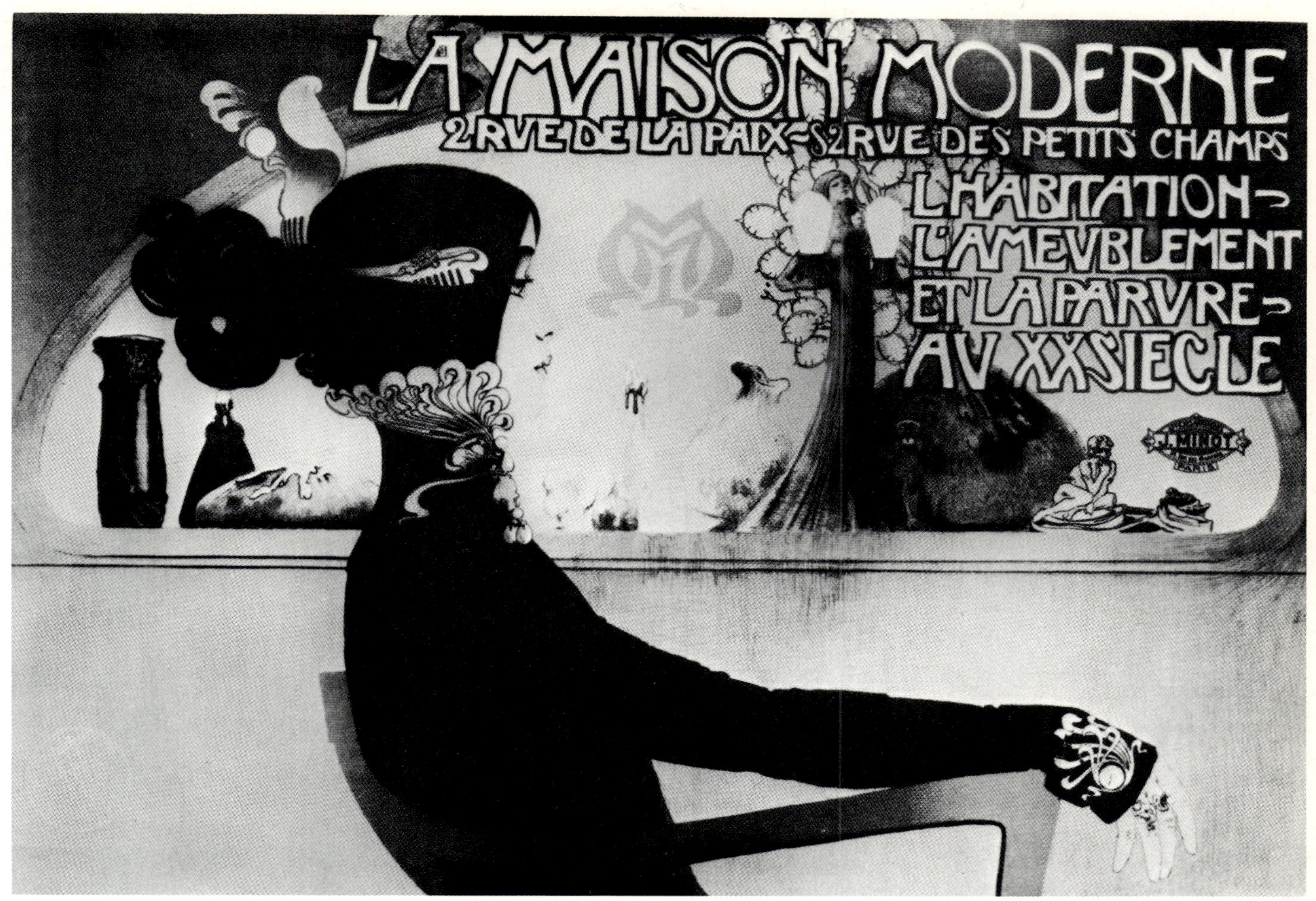


Manuel Orazi
*La Maison moderne* c 1905

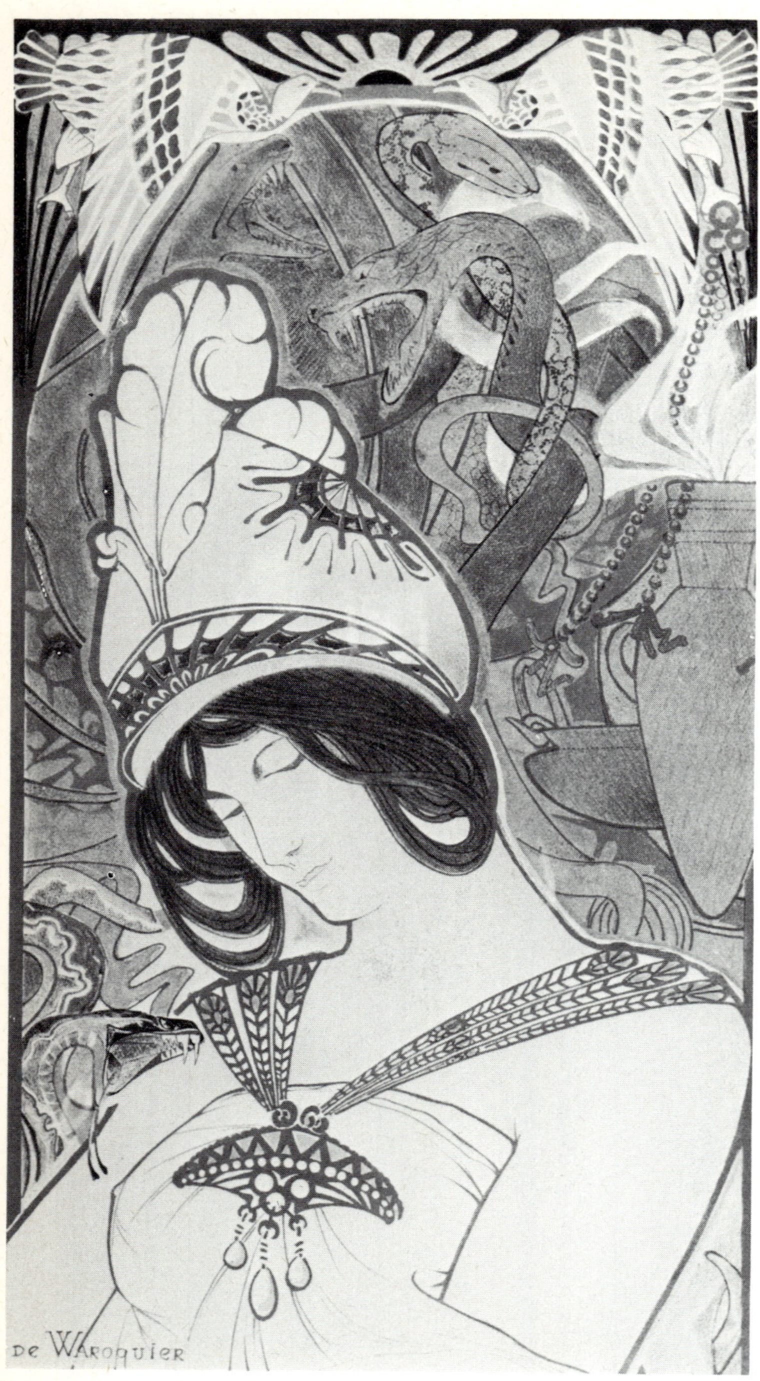


Henri de Waroquier
*Cléopâtre*

Richard Ranft
*L'Ecuyère* 1898

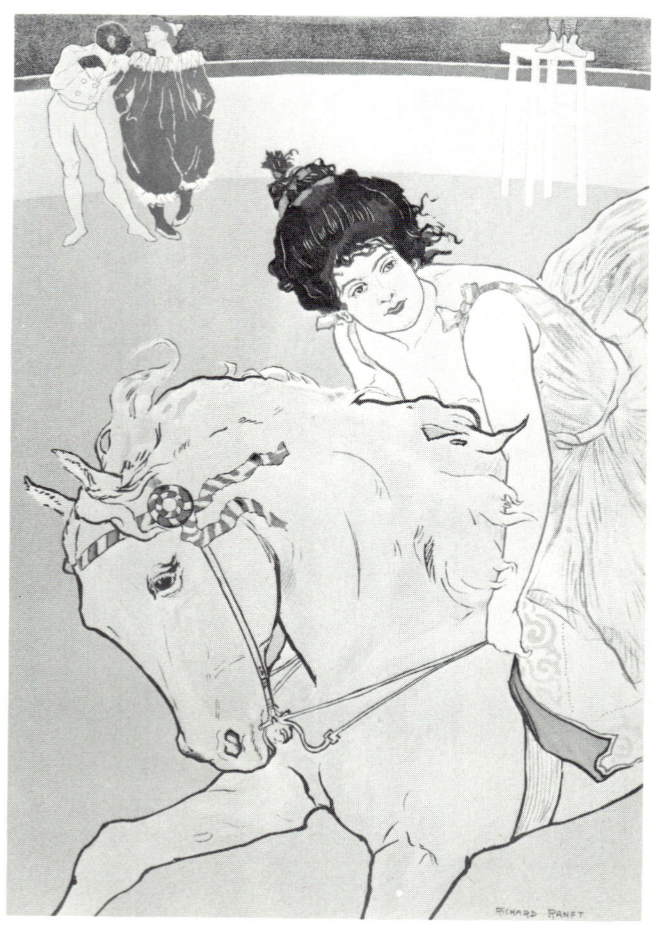

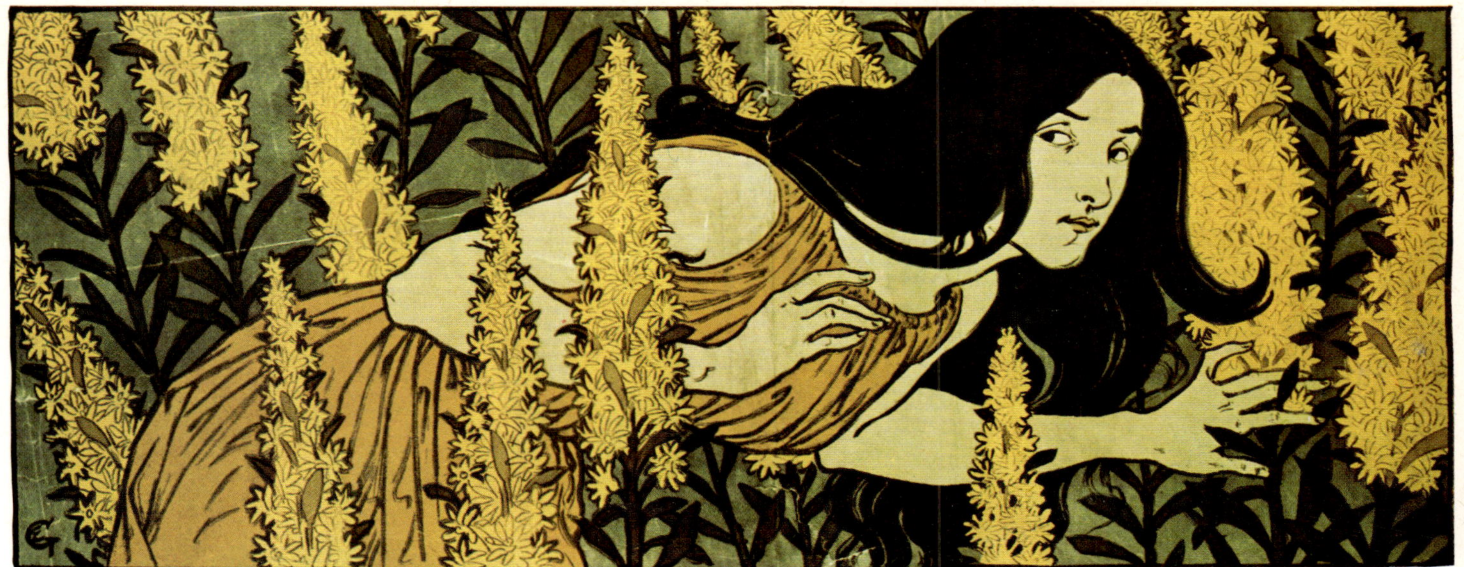

Eugène Grasset
*Dans les plantes*

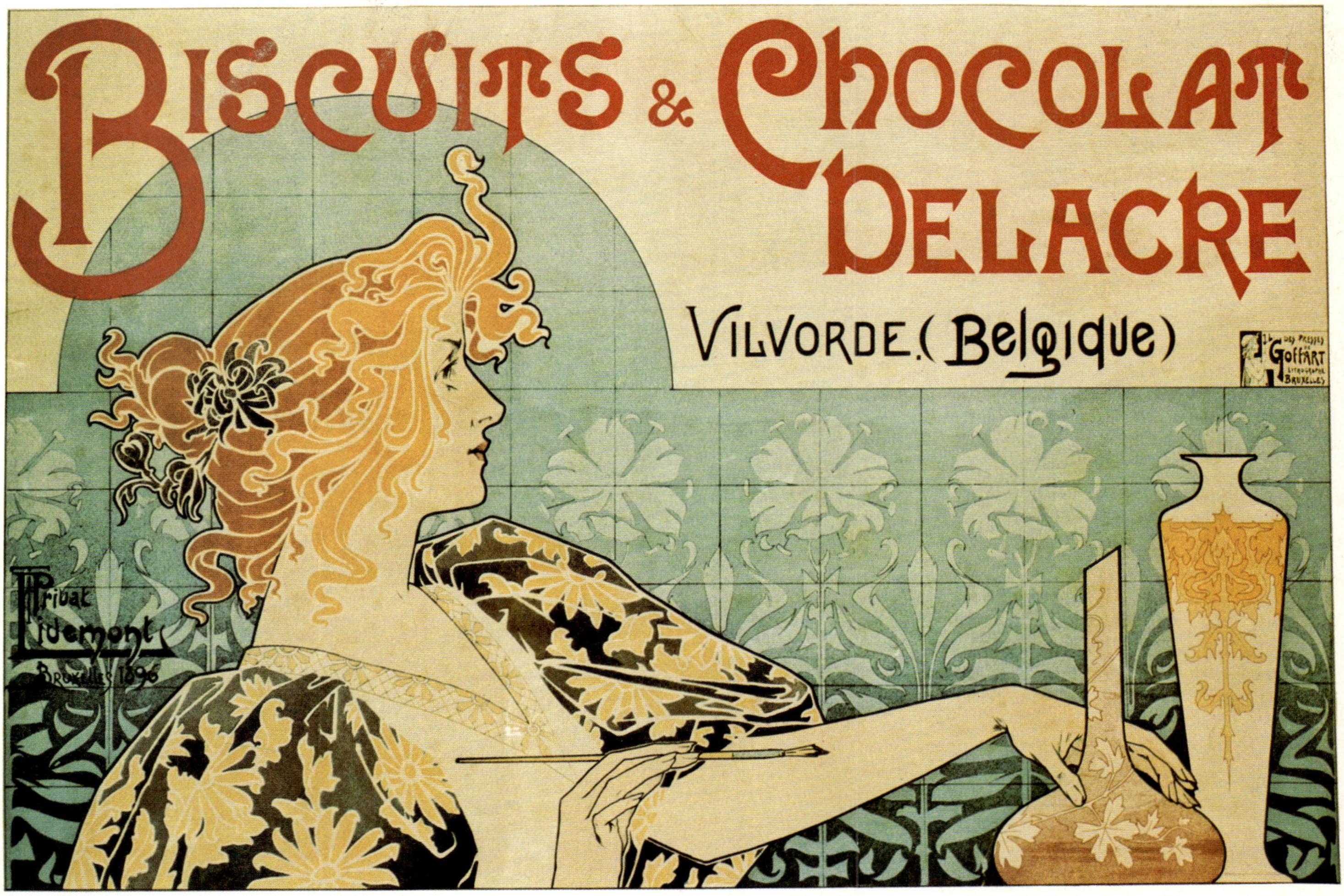

Privat Livemont
*Biscuits & chocolat Delacre* 1896

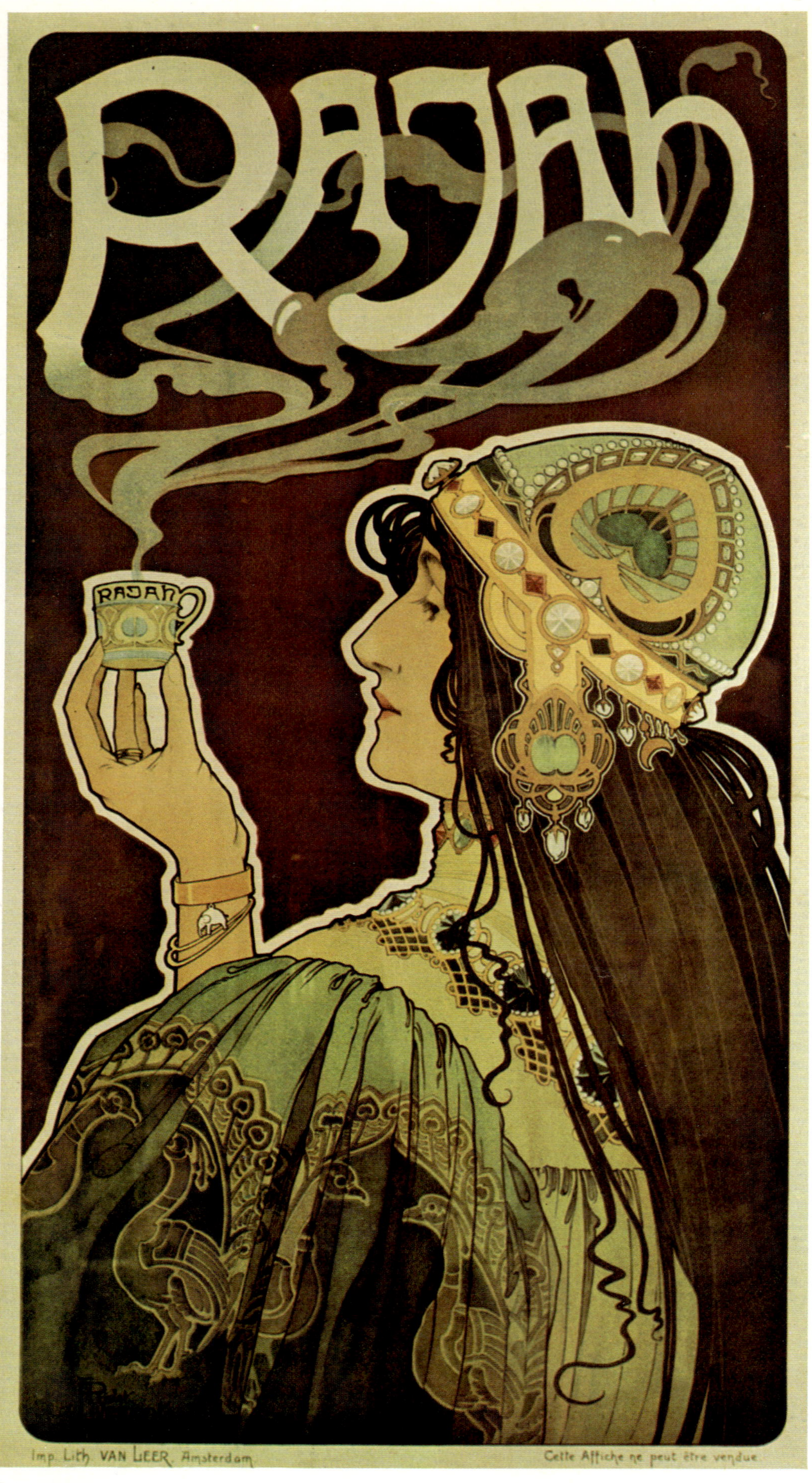


Privat Livemont
*Café Rajah* 1899

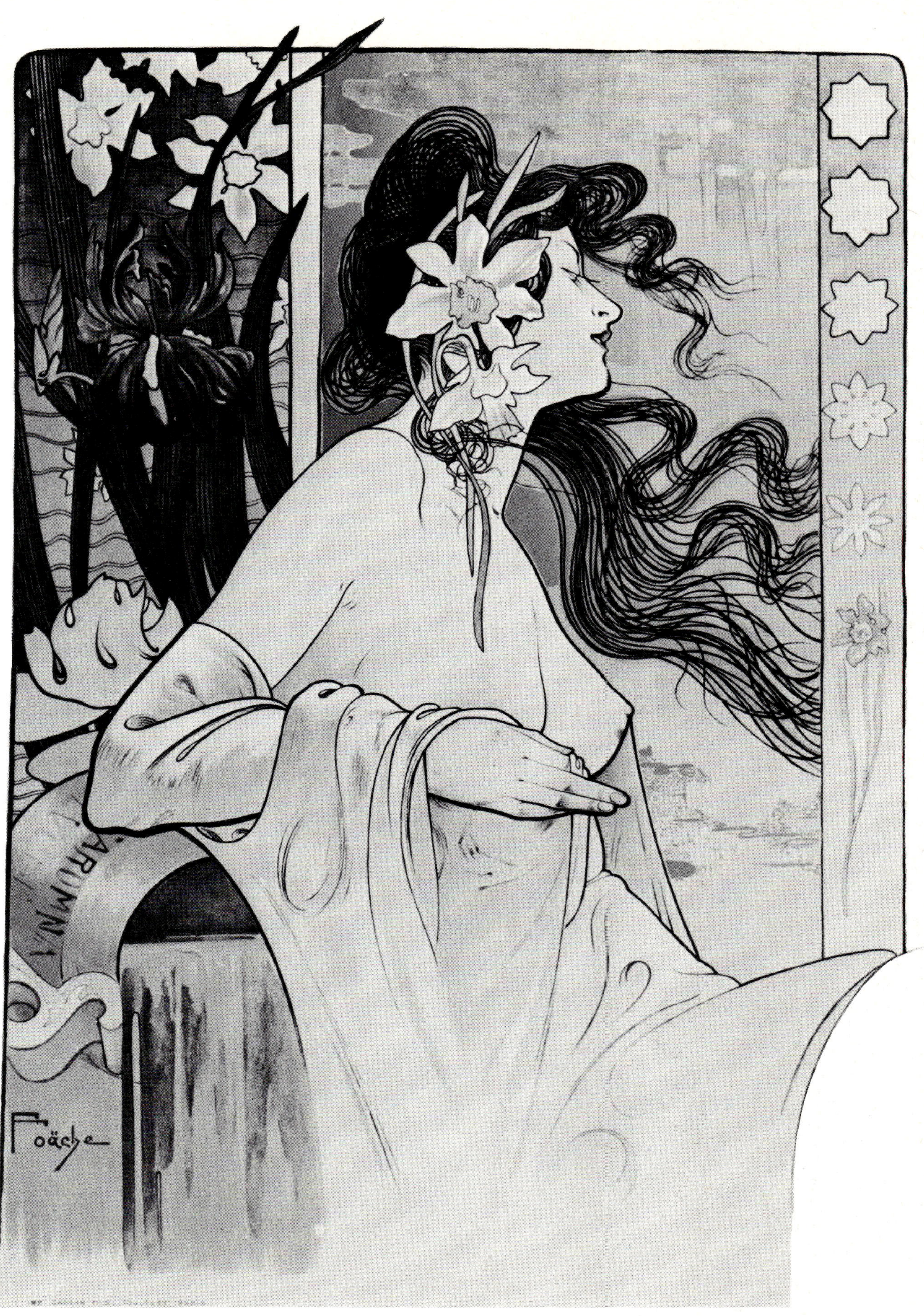


Foäche
*La Dépêche de Toulouse*

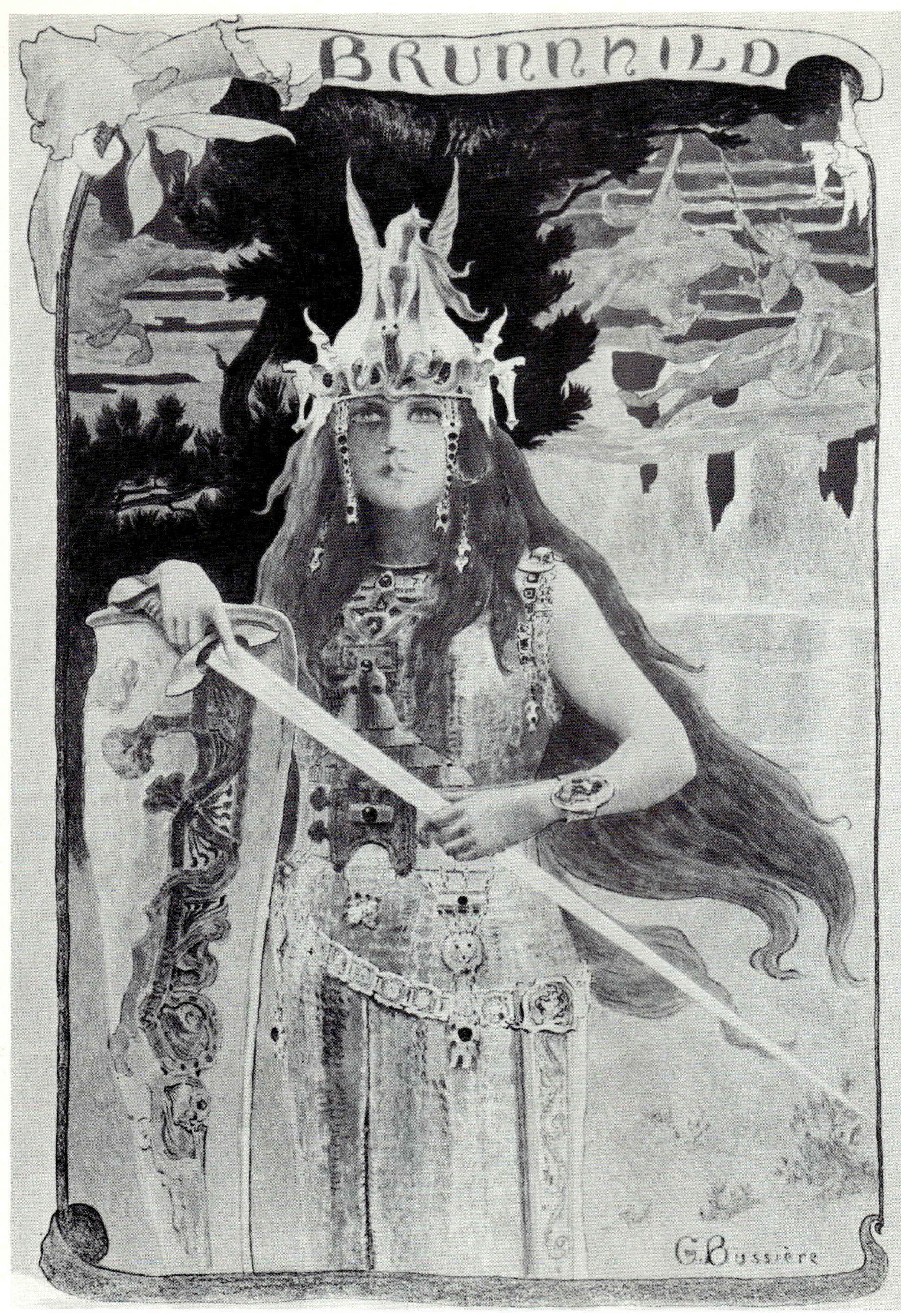


Gaston Bussière
*Brunnhild*

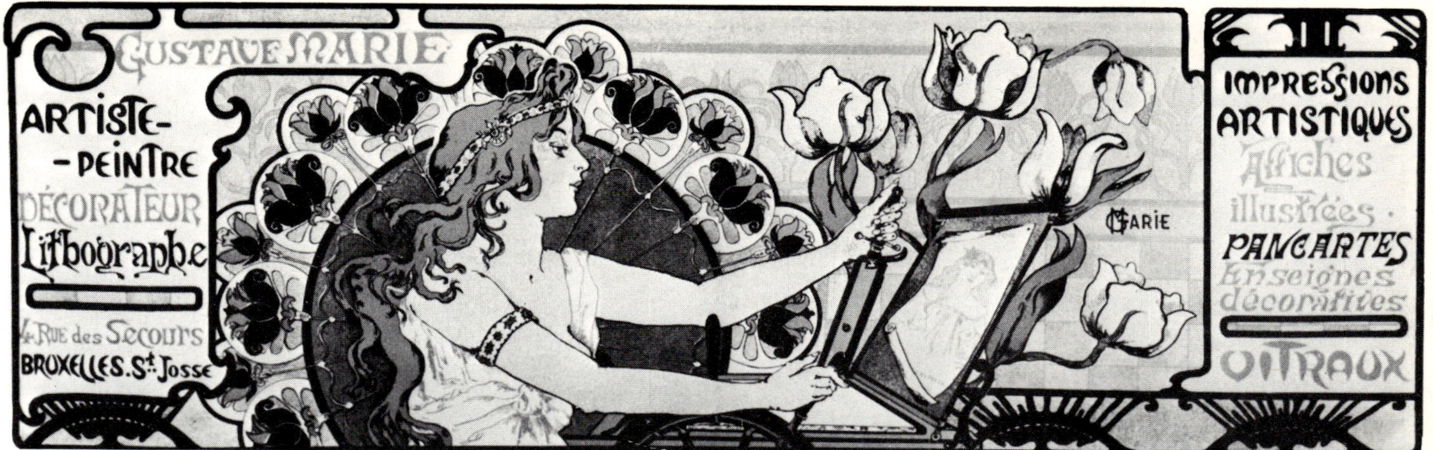


Gustave Marie
*Atelier Marie*

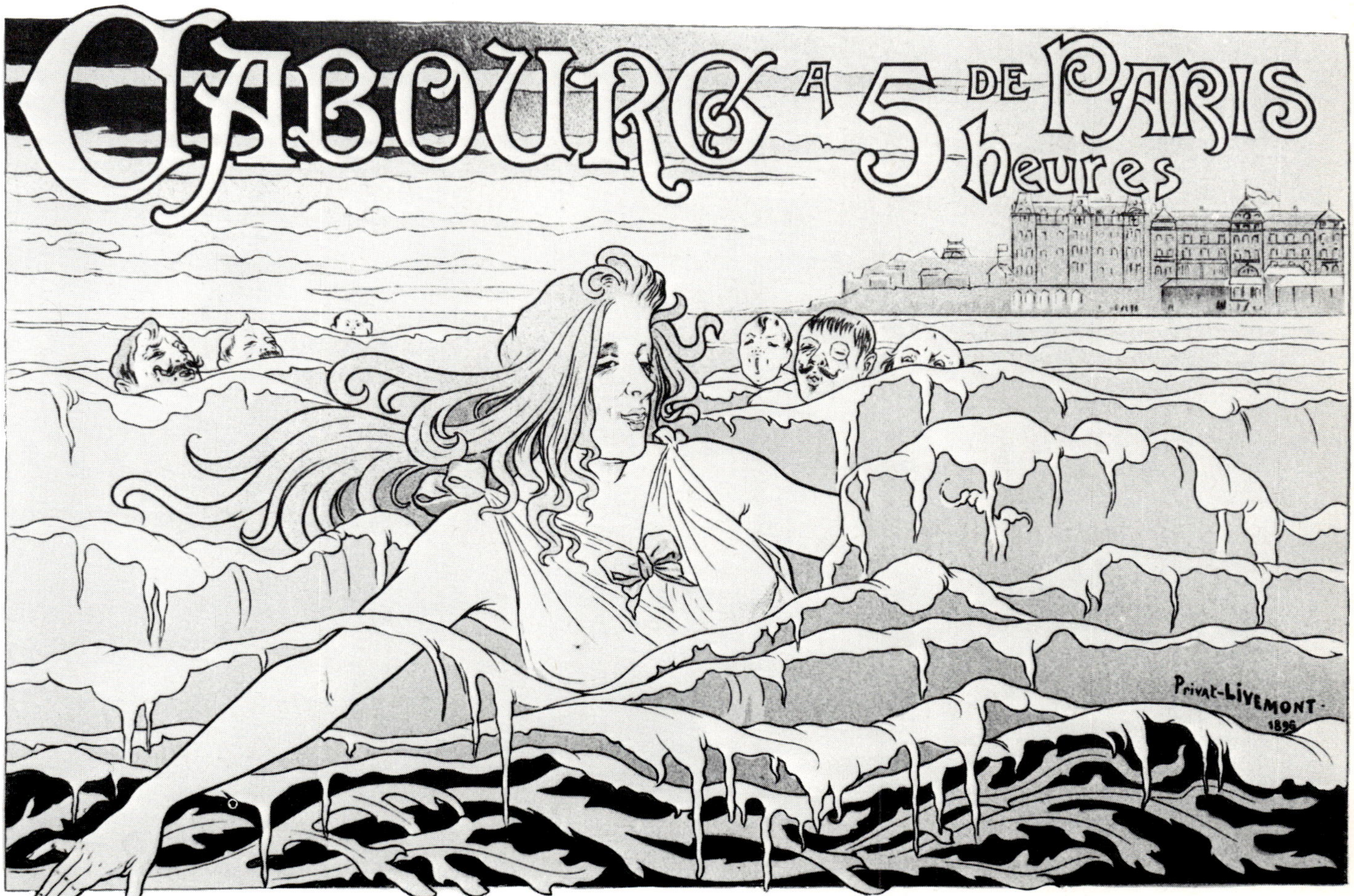

Privat Livemont
*Cabourg* 1896

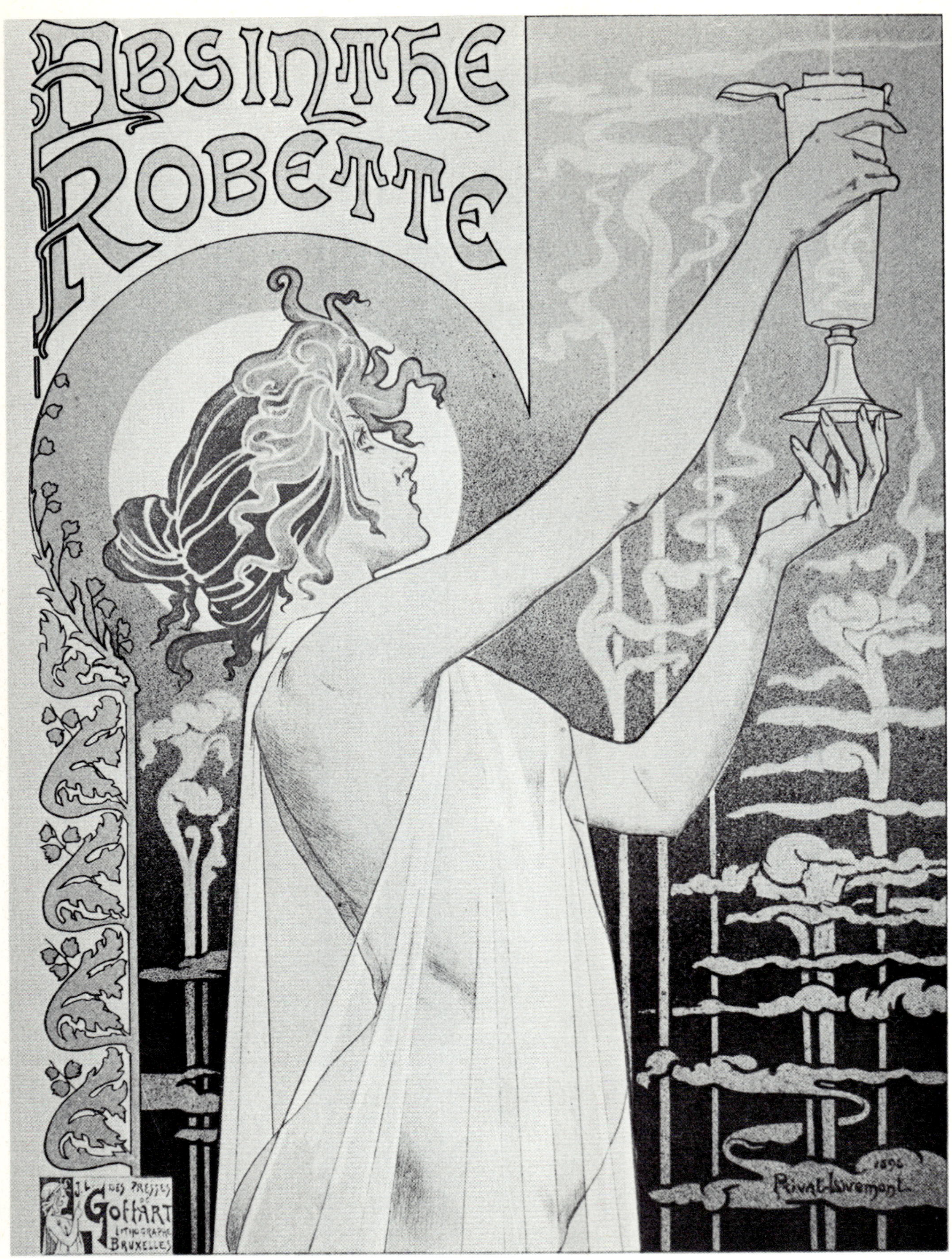


Privat Livemont
*Absinthe Robette* 1896

Privat Livemont
*Cercle artistique de Schaerbeek* 1897

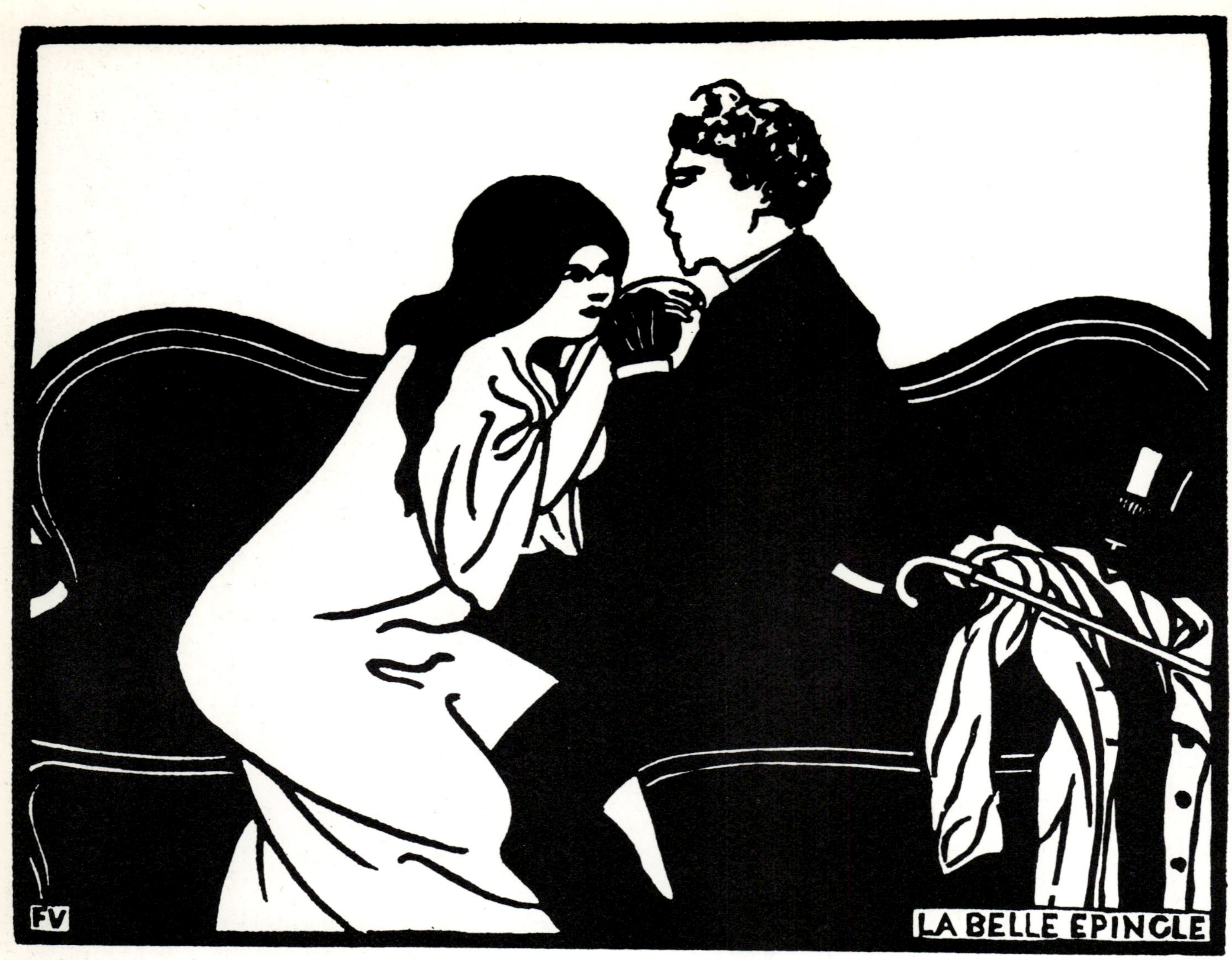


Félix Vallotton
*La belle épingle* 1897

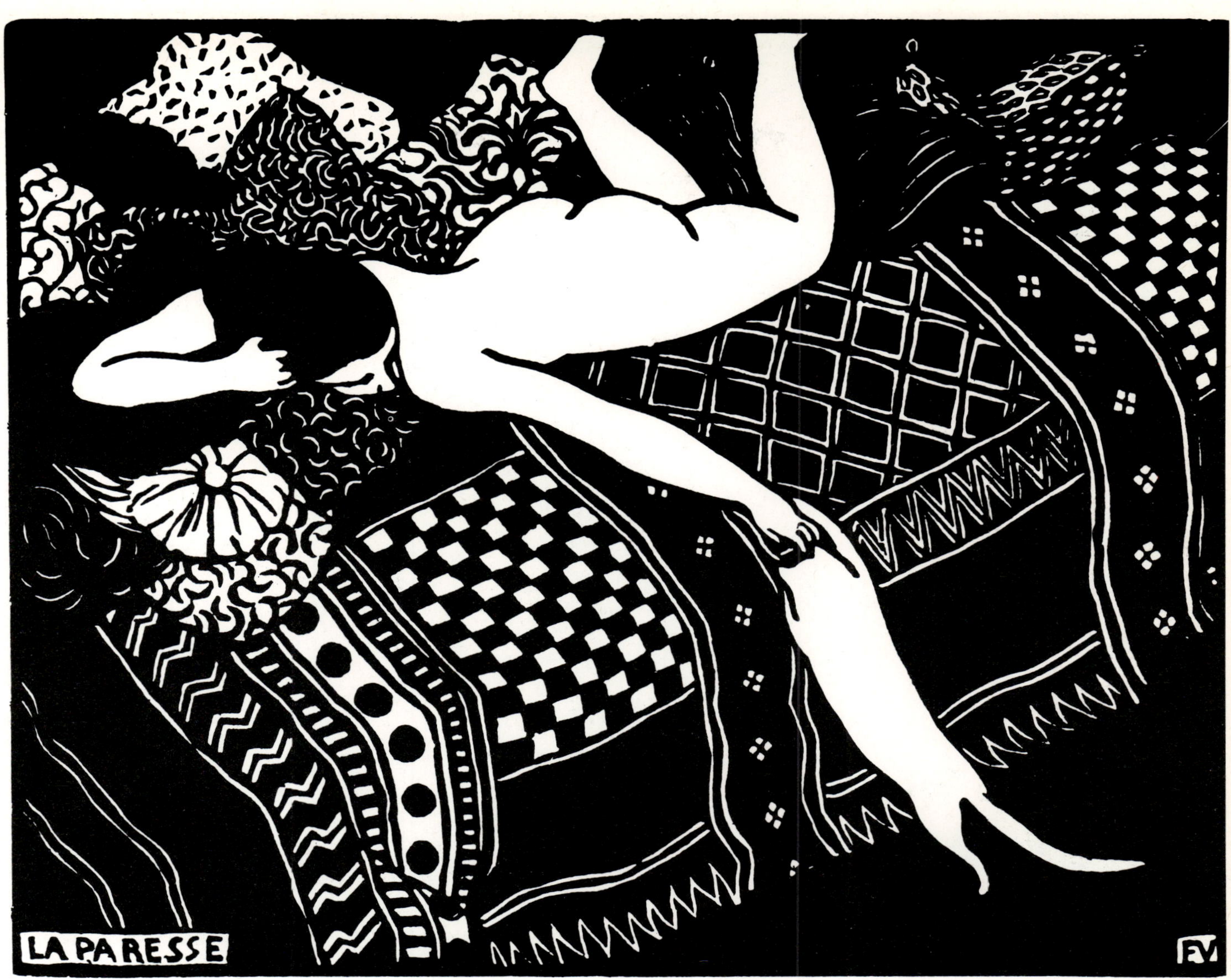


Félix Vallotton
*La Paresse* 1896

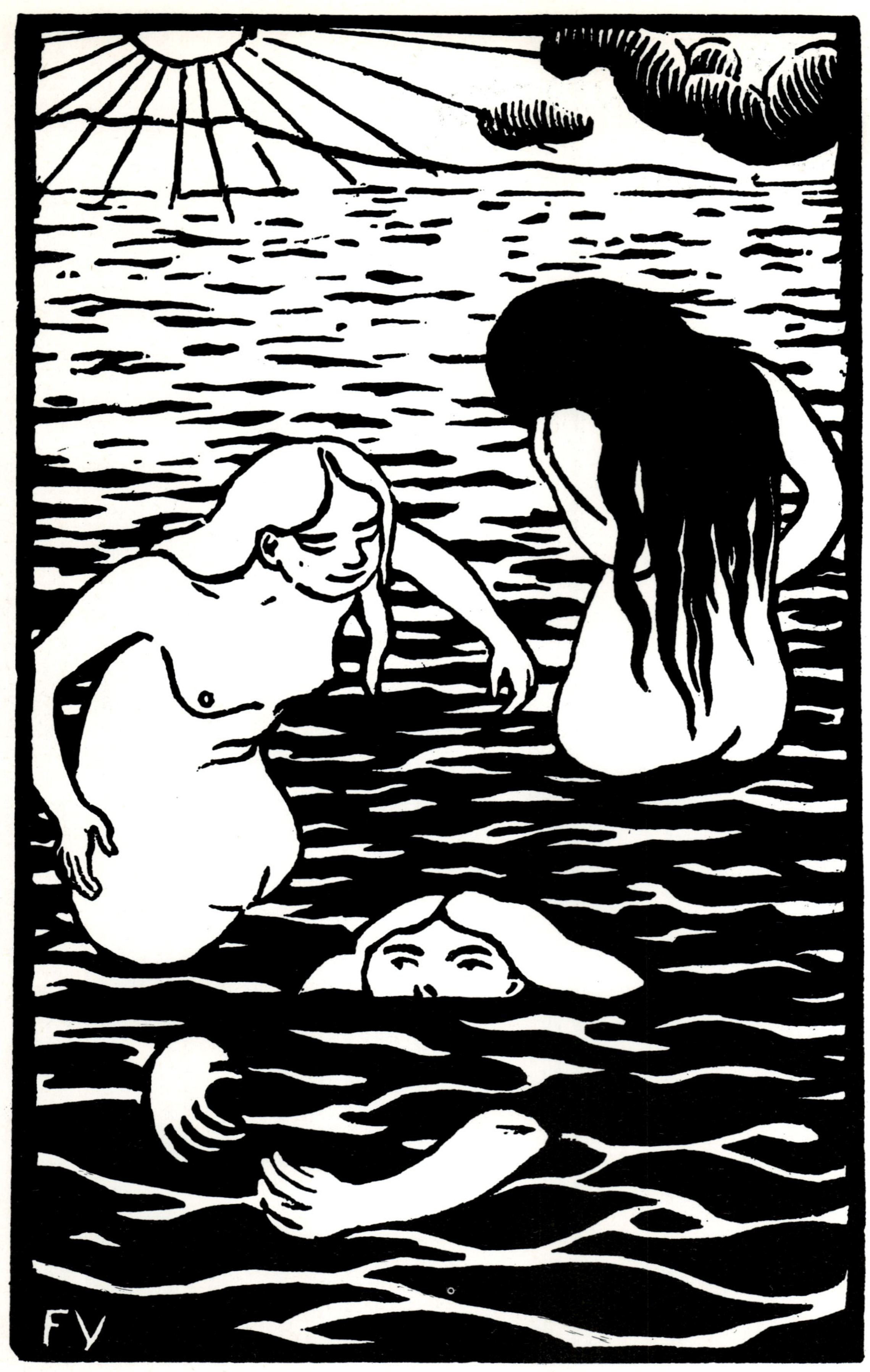


Félix Vallotton
*Trois baigneuses* 1894

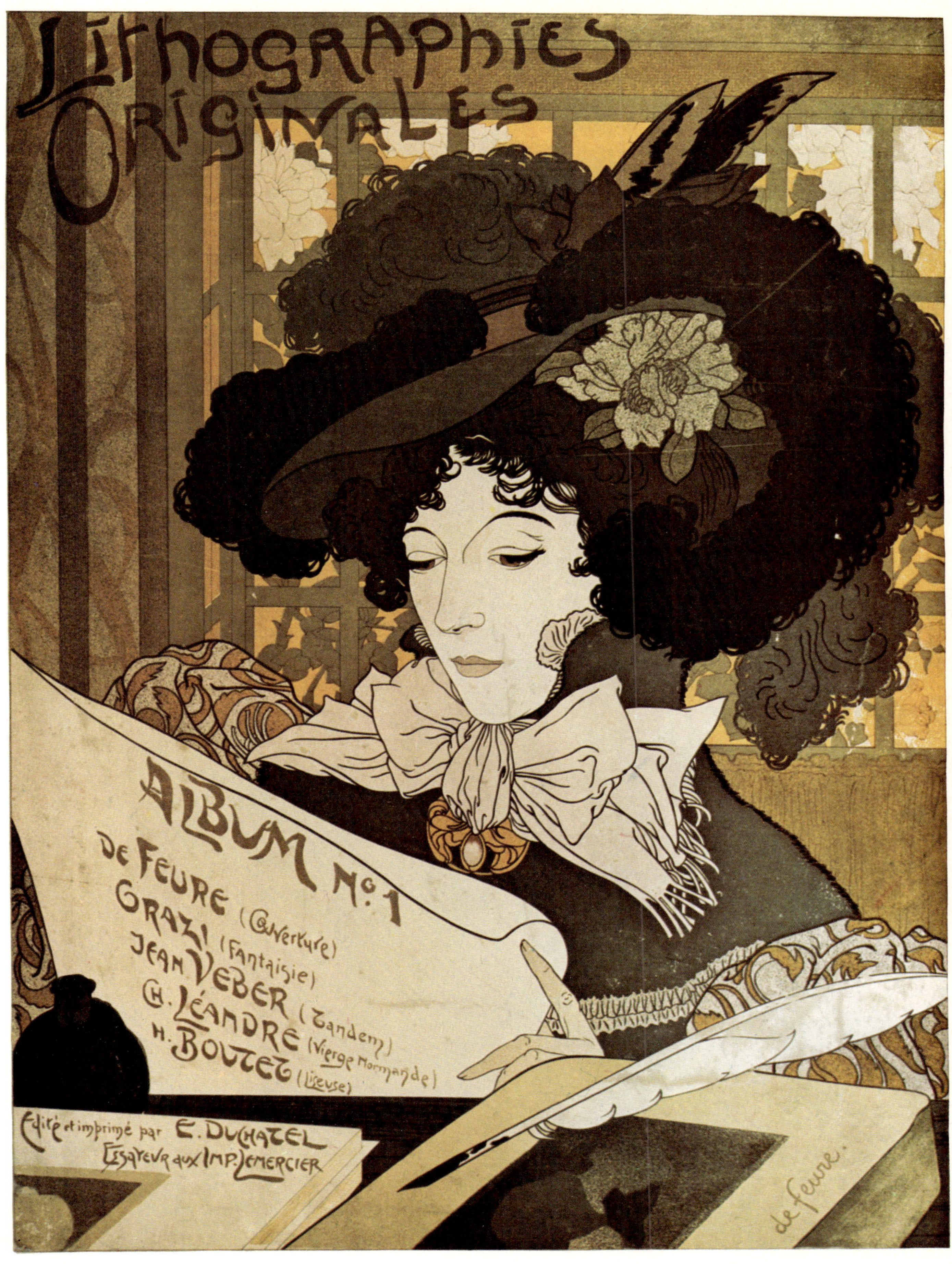


Georges de Feure
*Lithographies originales*

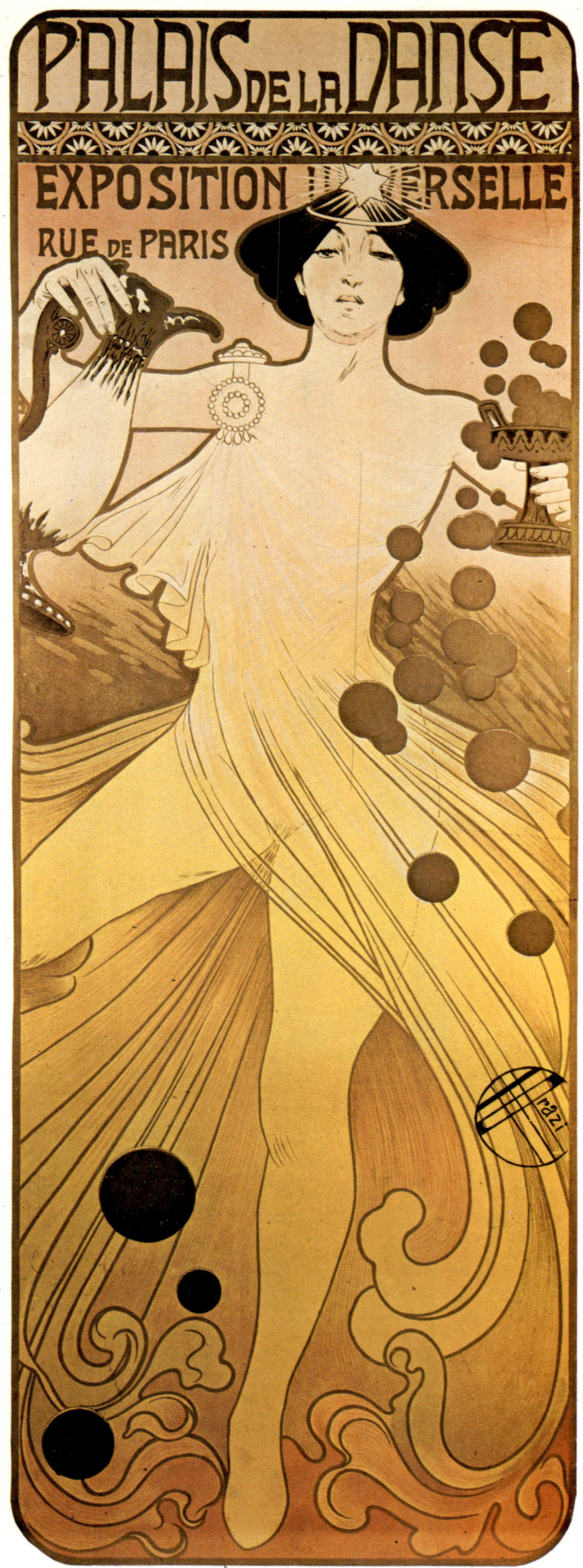


Manuel Orazi
*Palais de la Danse*

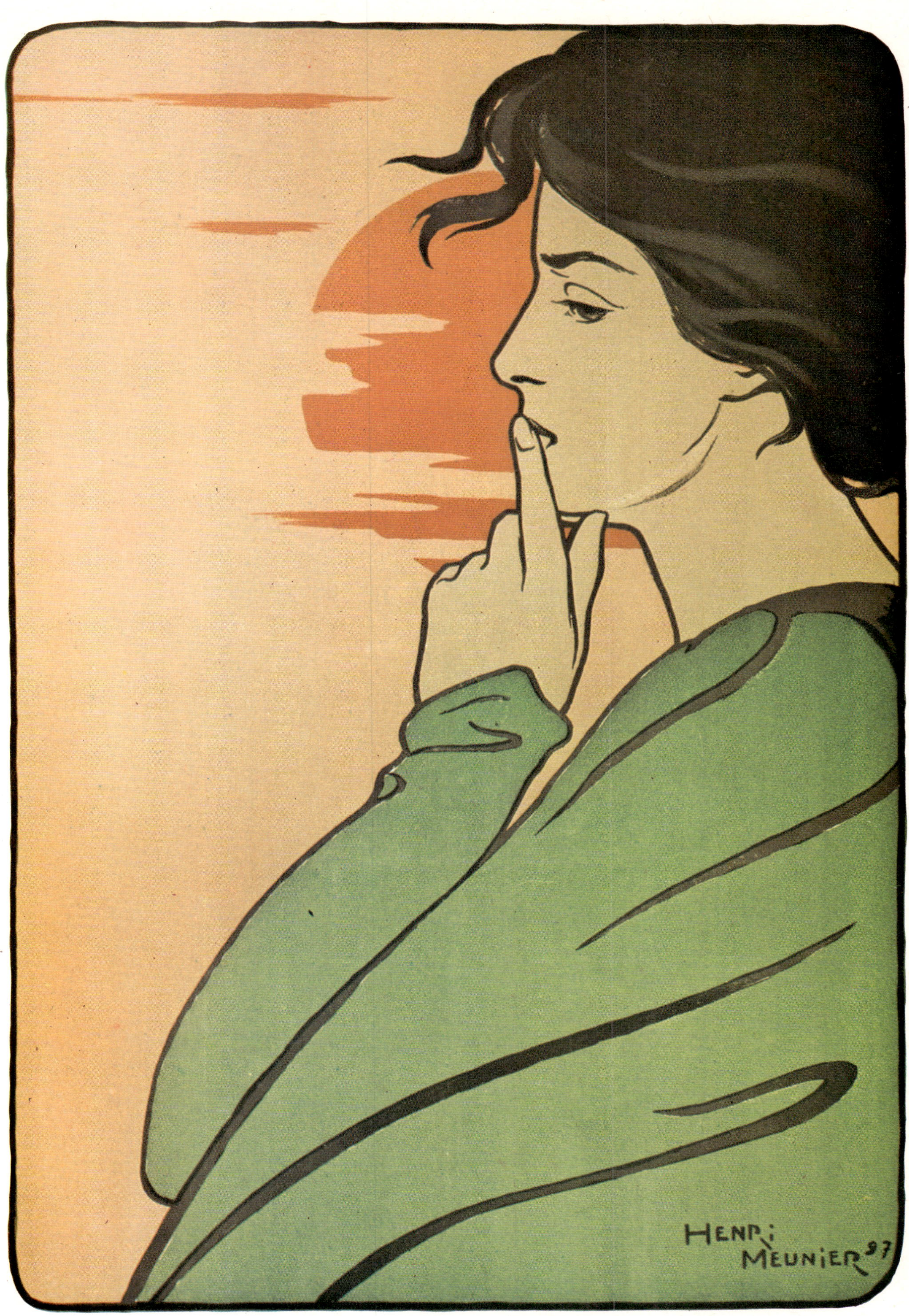


Henri Meunier
*L'Estampe moderne: L'Heure du silence* 1897

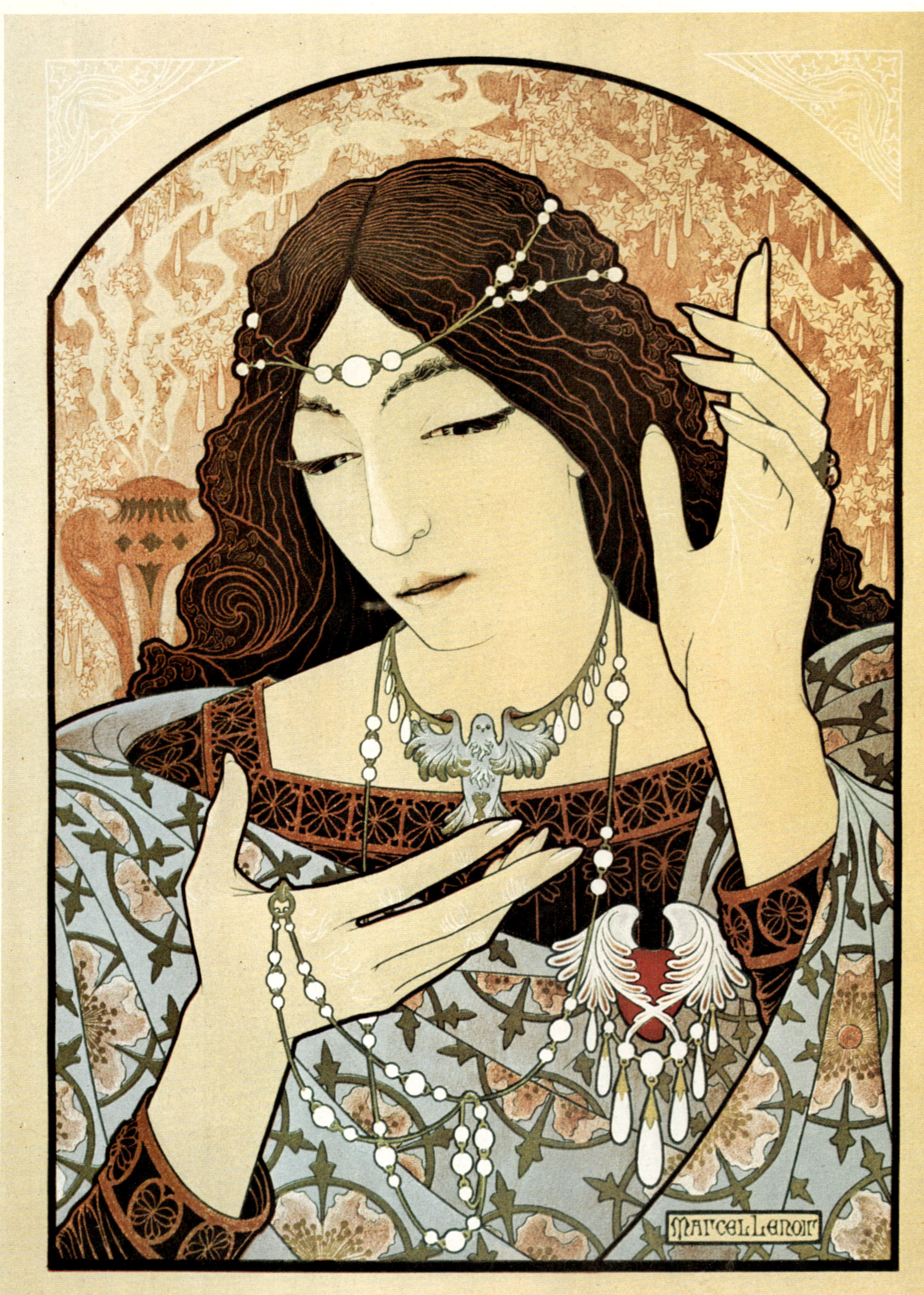


Marcel Lenoir
*L'Estampe moderne: Invocation à la madone d'onyx vert* 1897

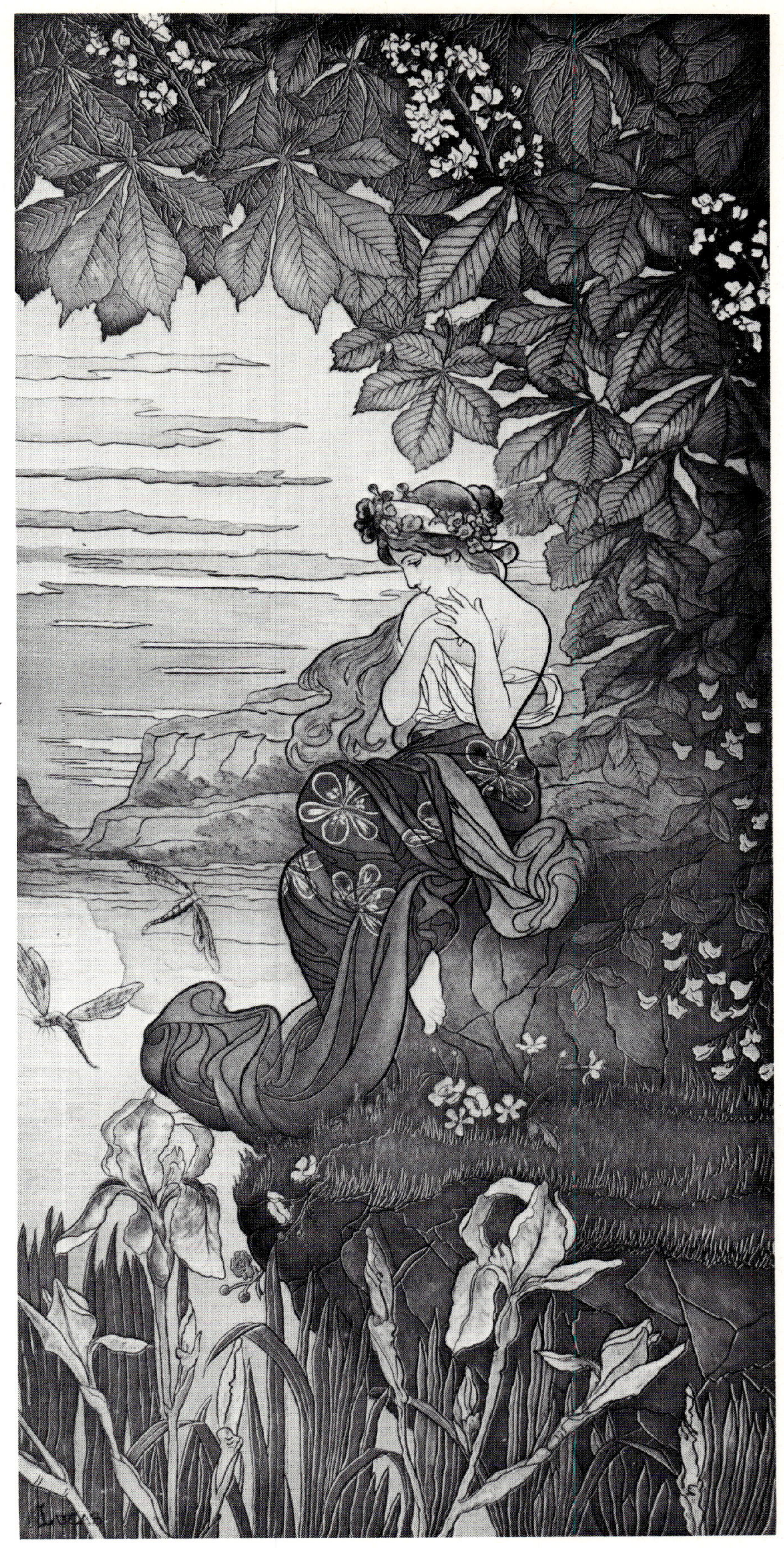

Hippolyte Lucas
*La Femme aux iris*

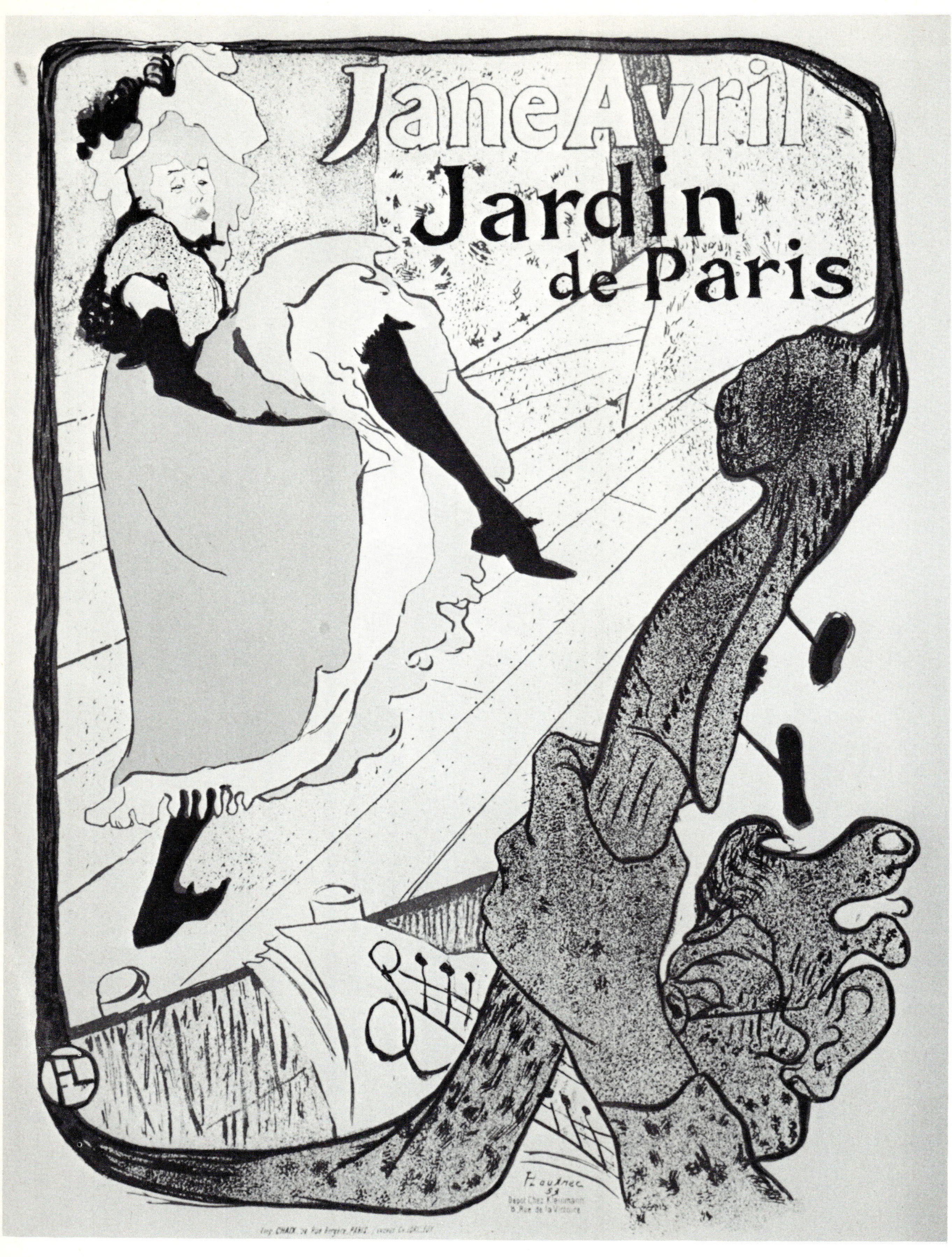


Henri de Toulouse-Lautrec
*Jane Avril* 1893

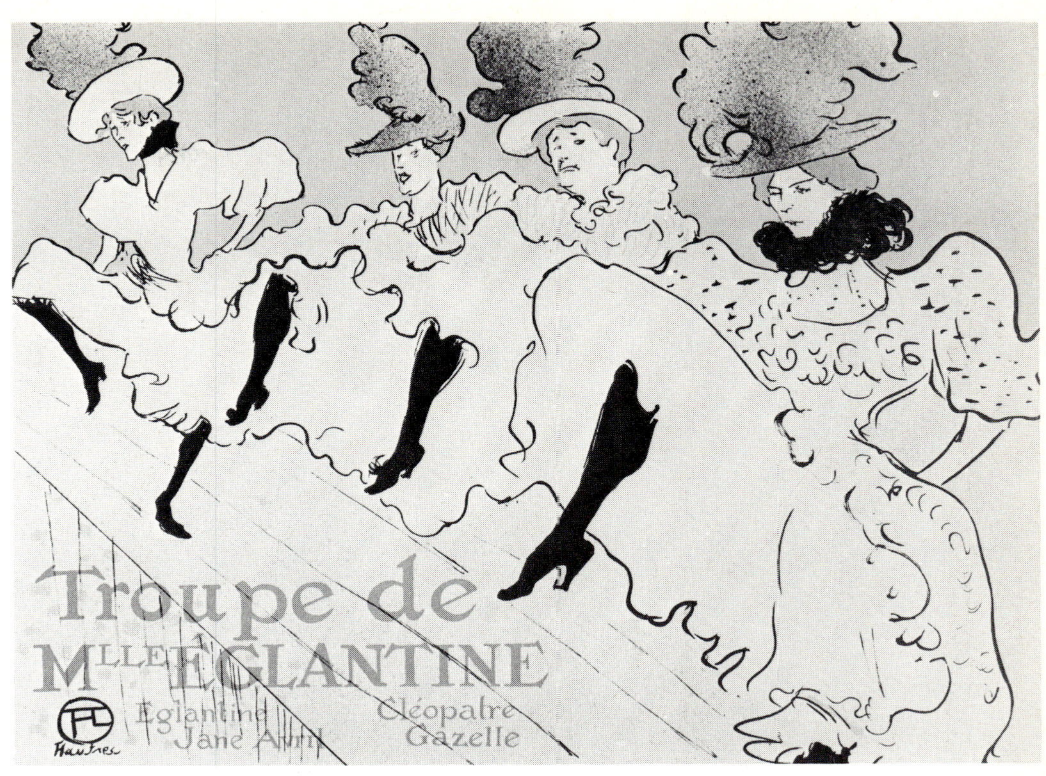


Henri de Toulouse-Lautrec
*La Troupe de Mademoiselle Eglantine* 1896

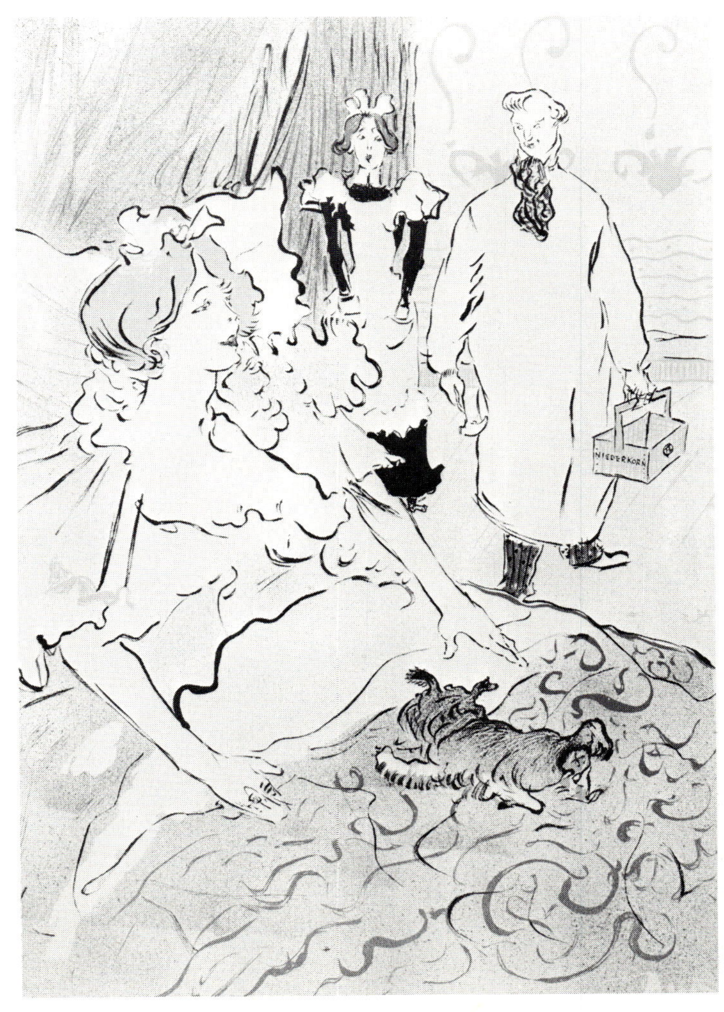

Henri de Toulouse-Lautrec
*L'Artisan moderne* (detail) 1894

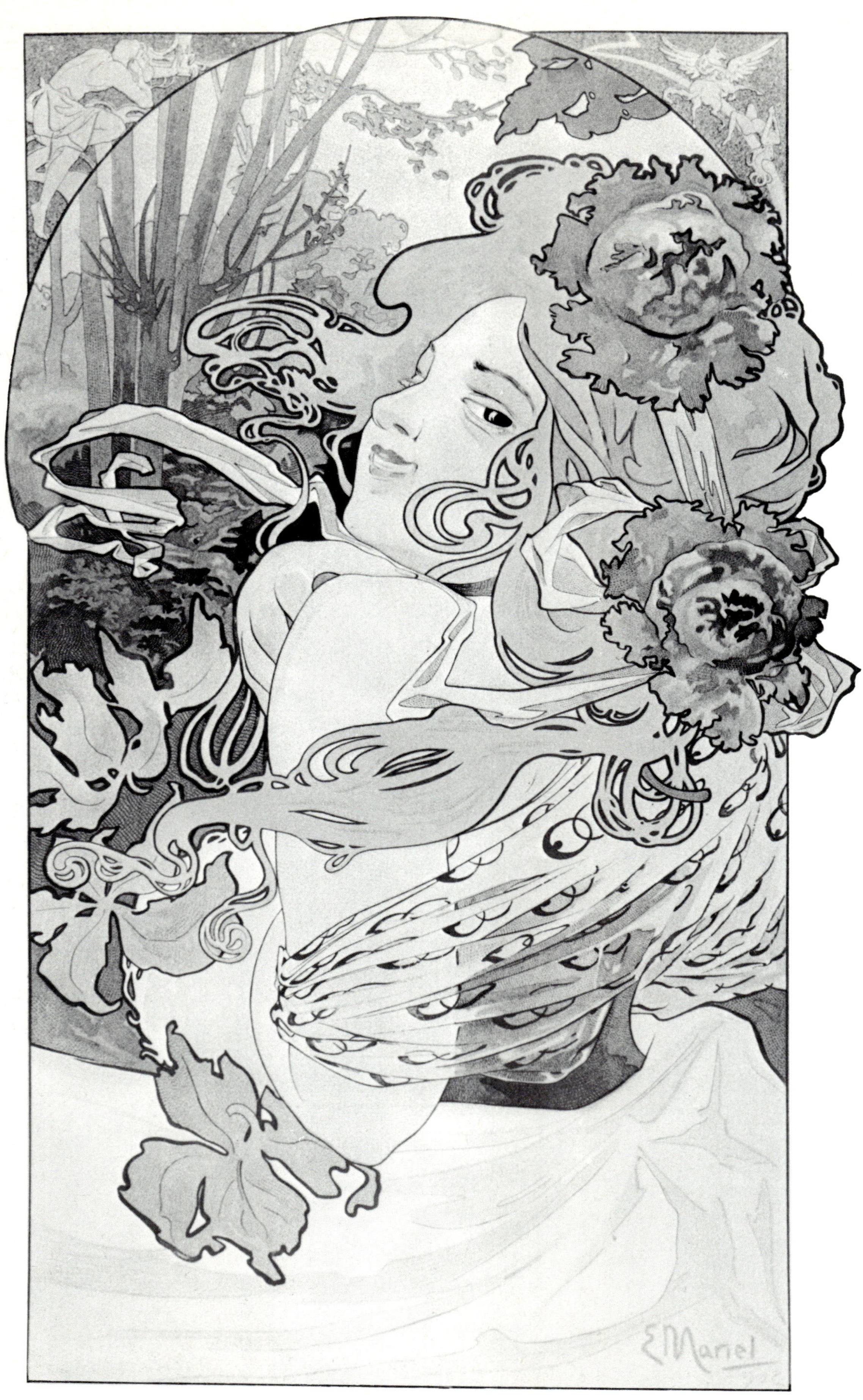


E. Mariel
*Coquelicots*

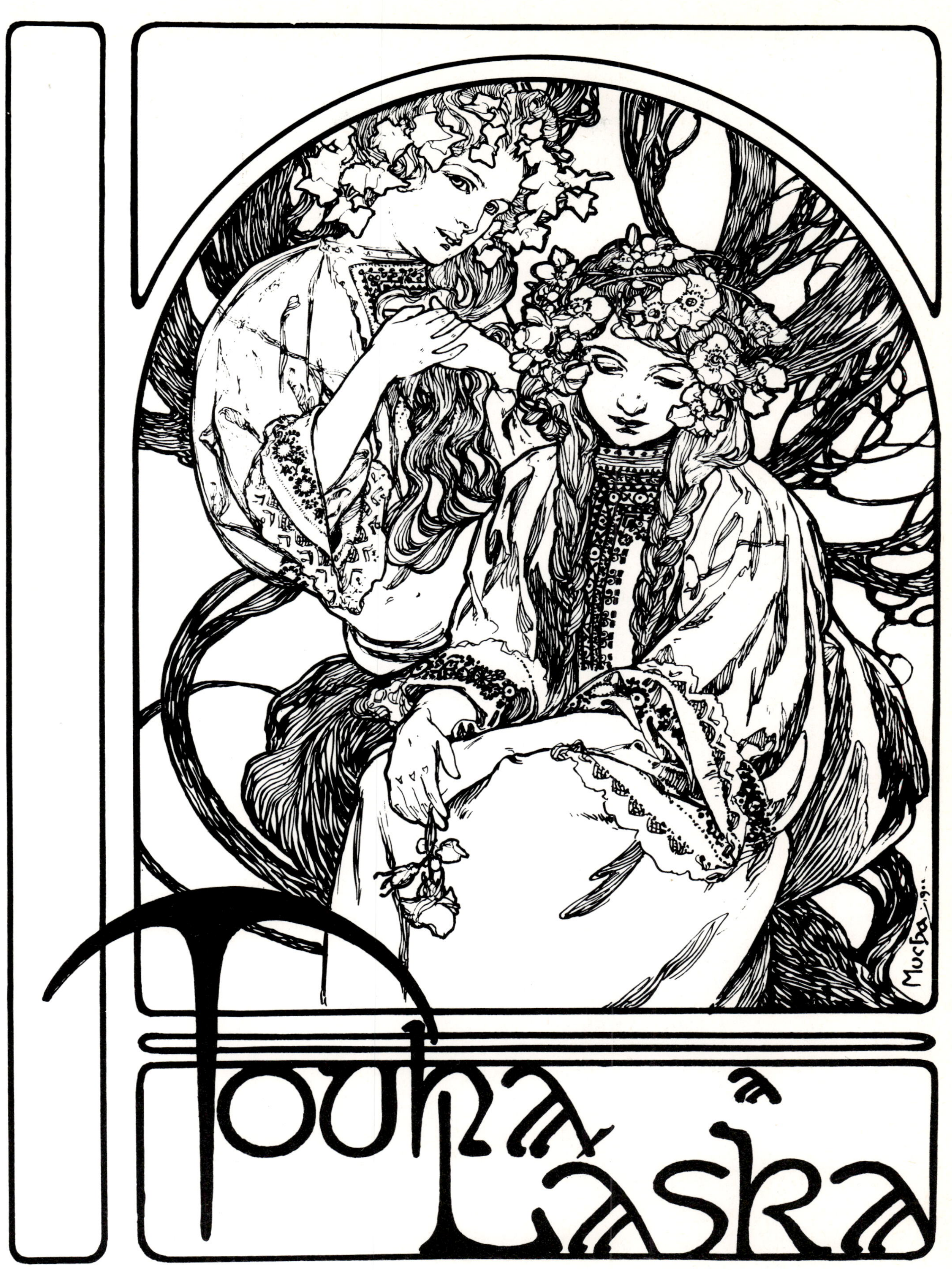


Alphonse Mucha
*Touha a Laska* c 1902

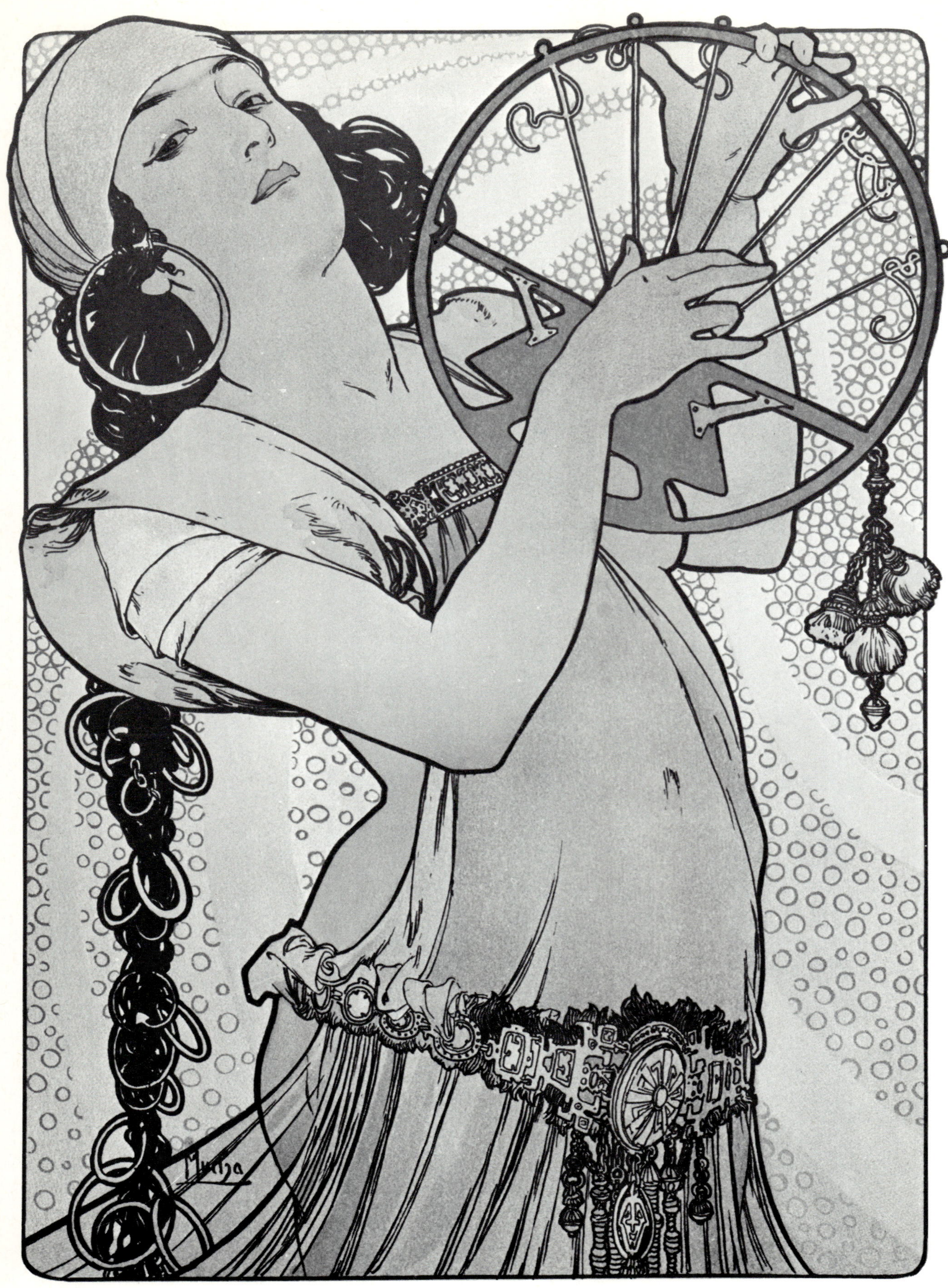


Alphonse Mucha
*L'Estampe moderne: Salomé* 1897

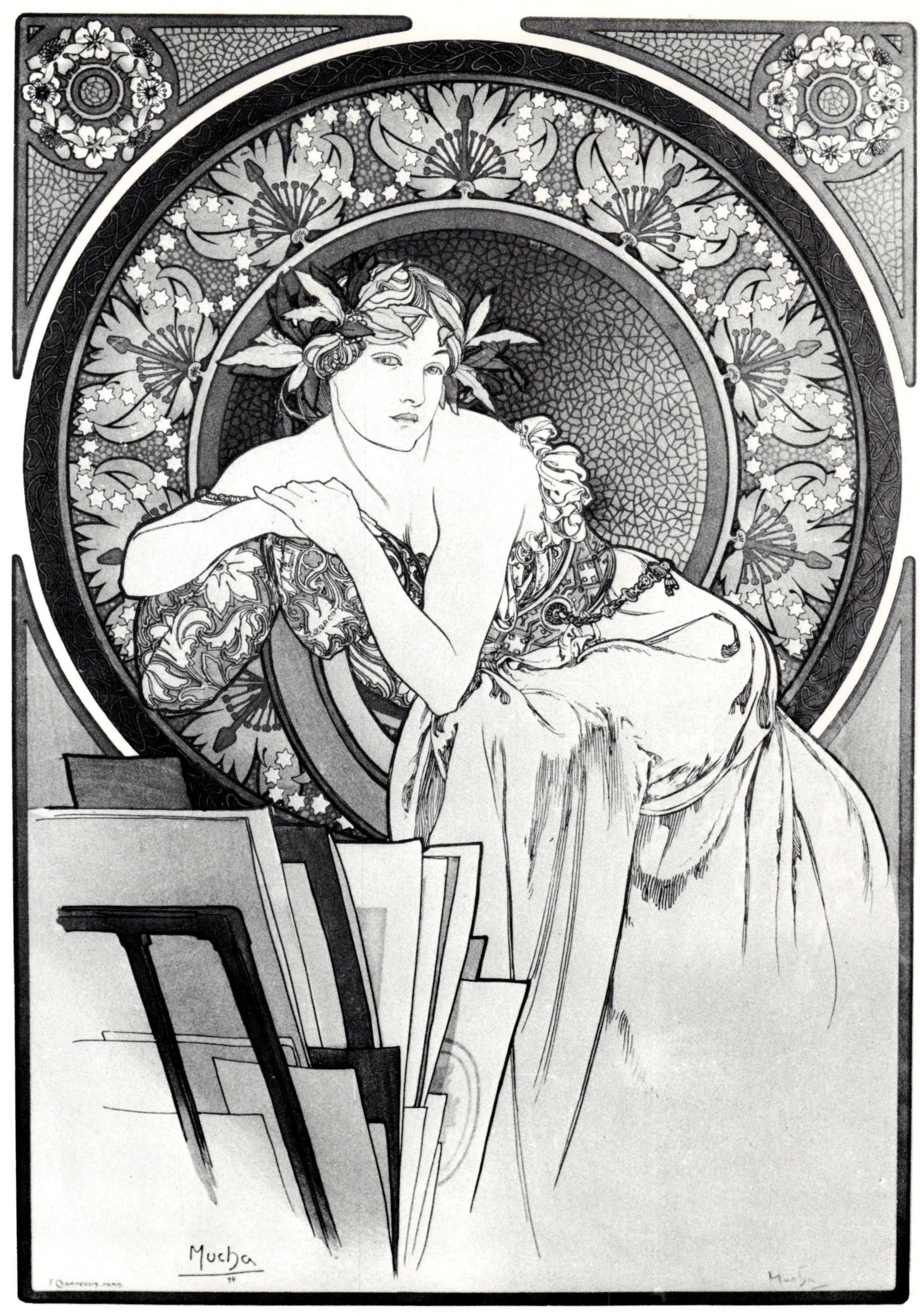


Alphonse Mucha
*Femme au chevalet* 1898

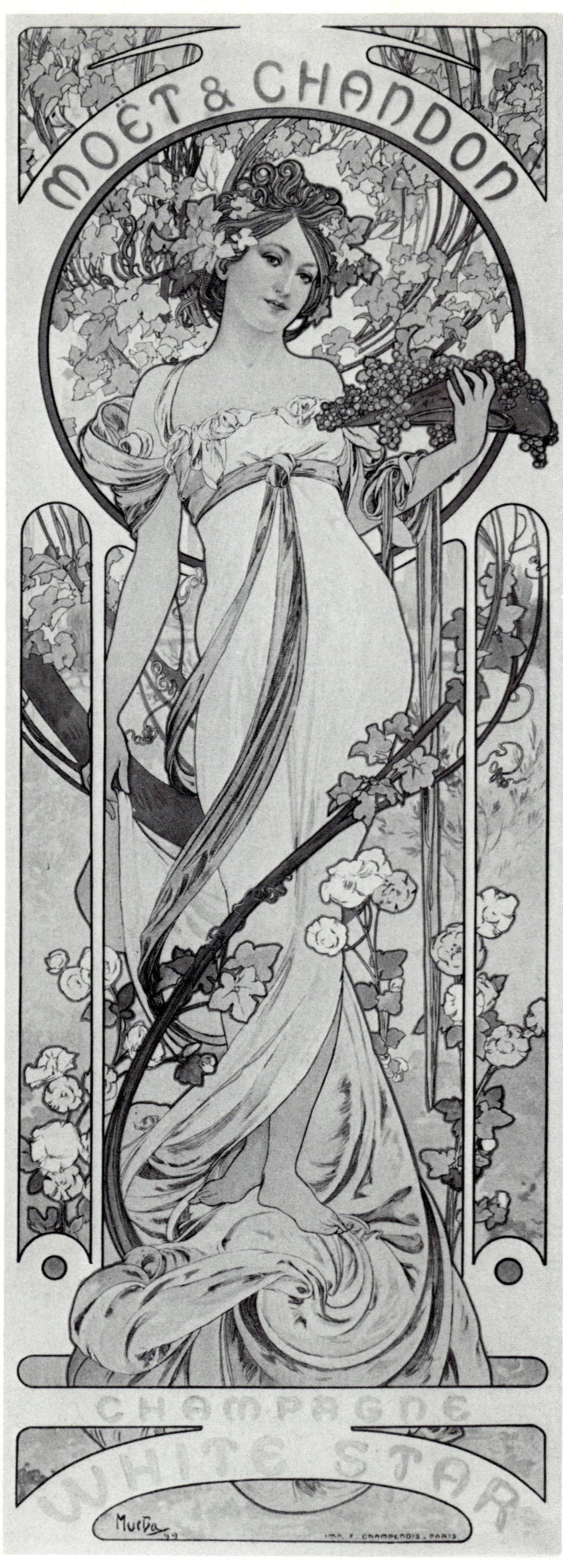


Alphonse Mucha
*Moët & Chandon* 1899

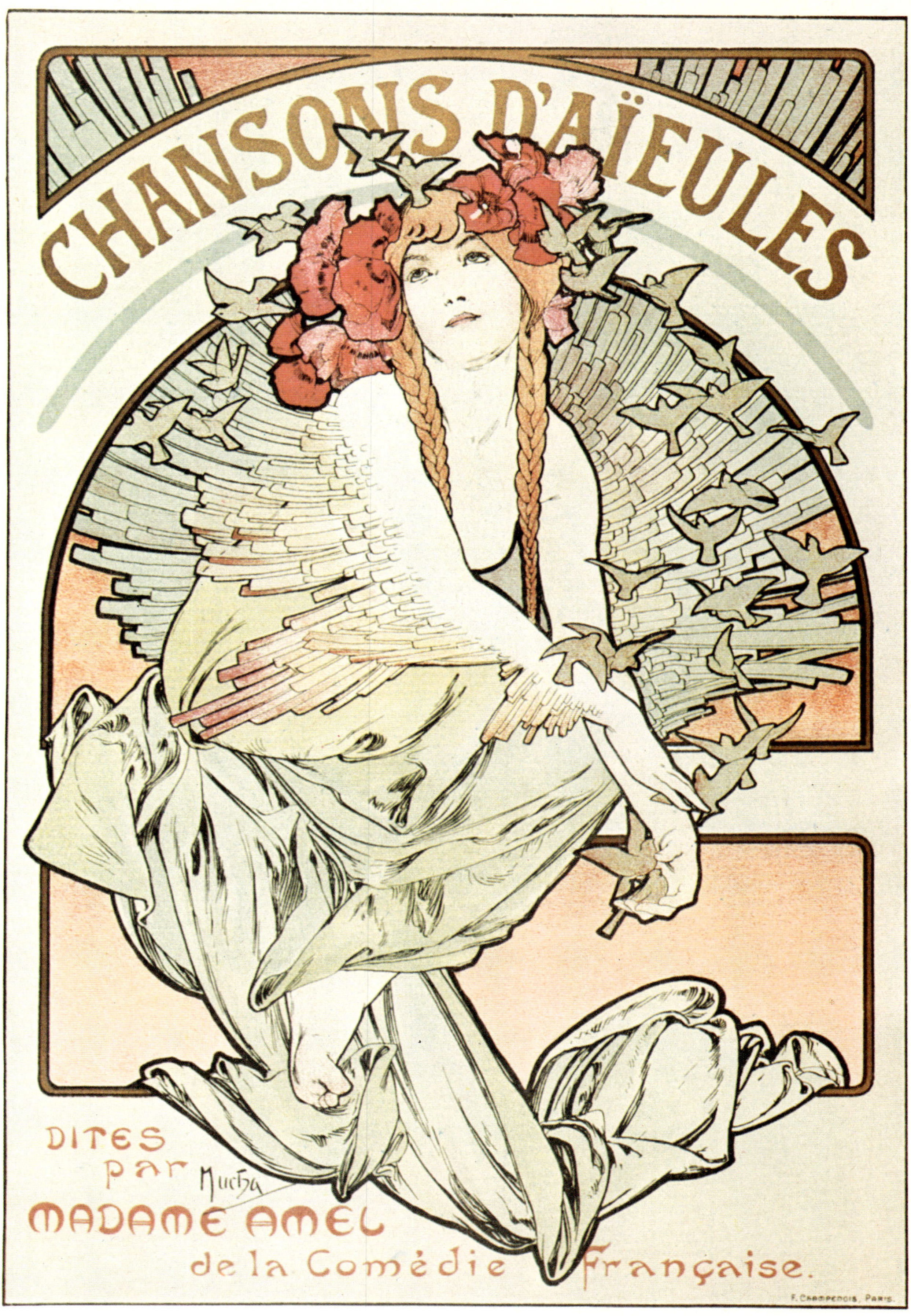


Alphonse Mucha
*Chansons d'aïeules* c 1898

Gisbert Combaz
*La Libre Esthétique Salon annuel* 1899

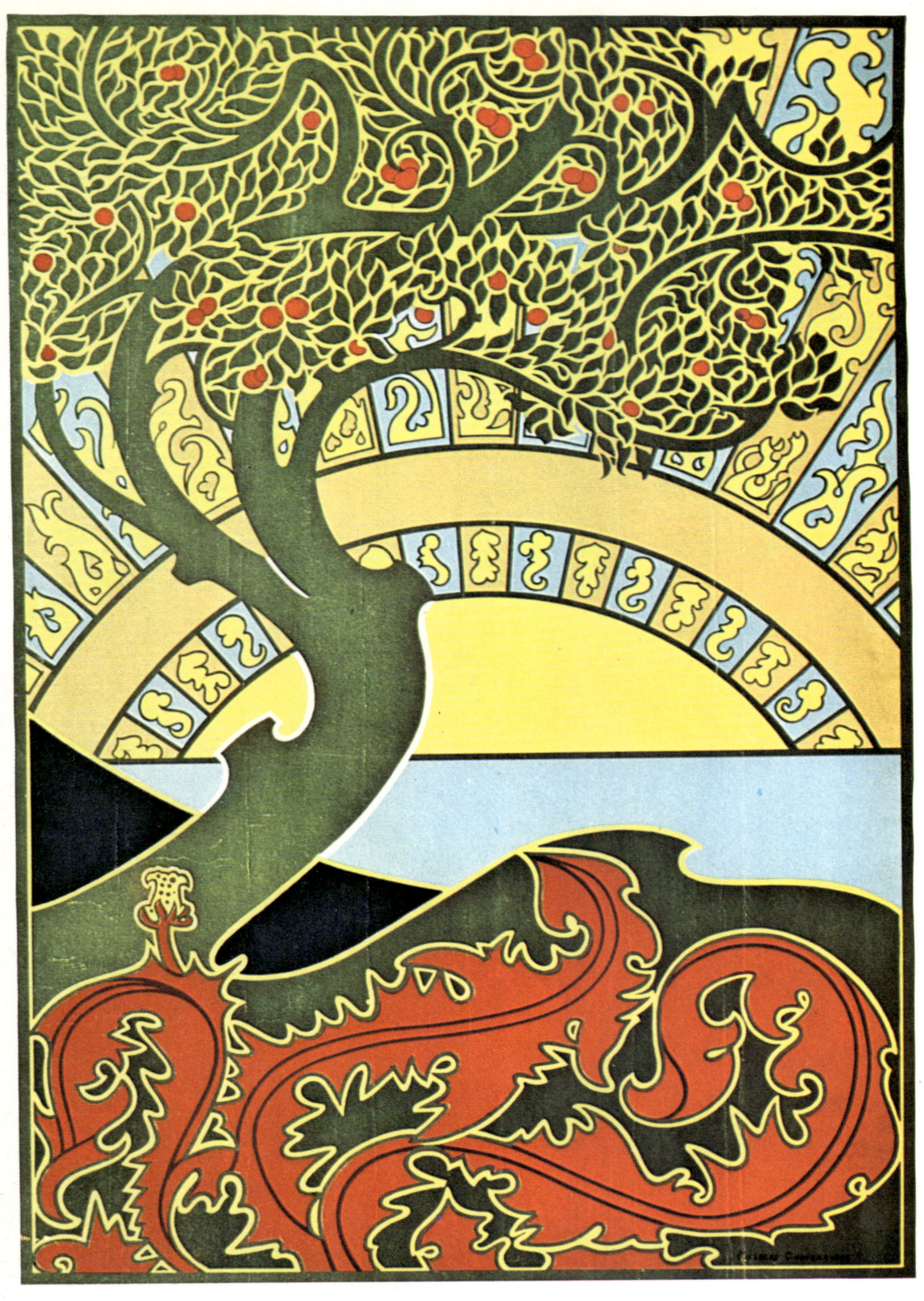

LA LIBRE ESTHETIQUE
SALON ANNUEL: MUSEE
MODERNE: DE 10 A 5 H S OU
VERTURE: 23 FEVRIER
PRIX D'ENTREE: 1 FR LE DIMANCHE 50 C

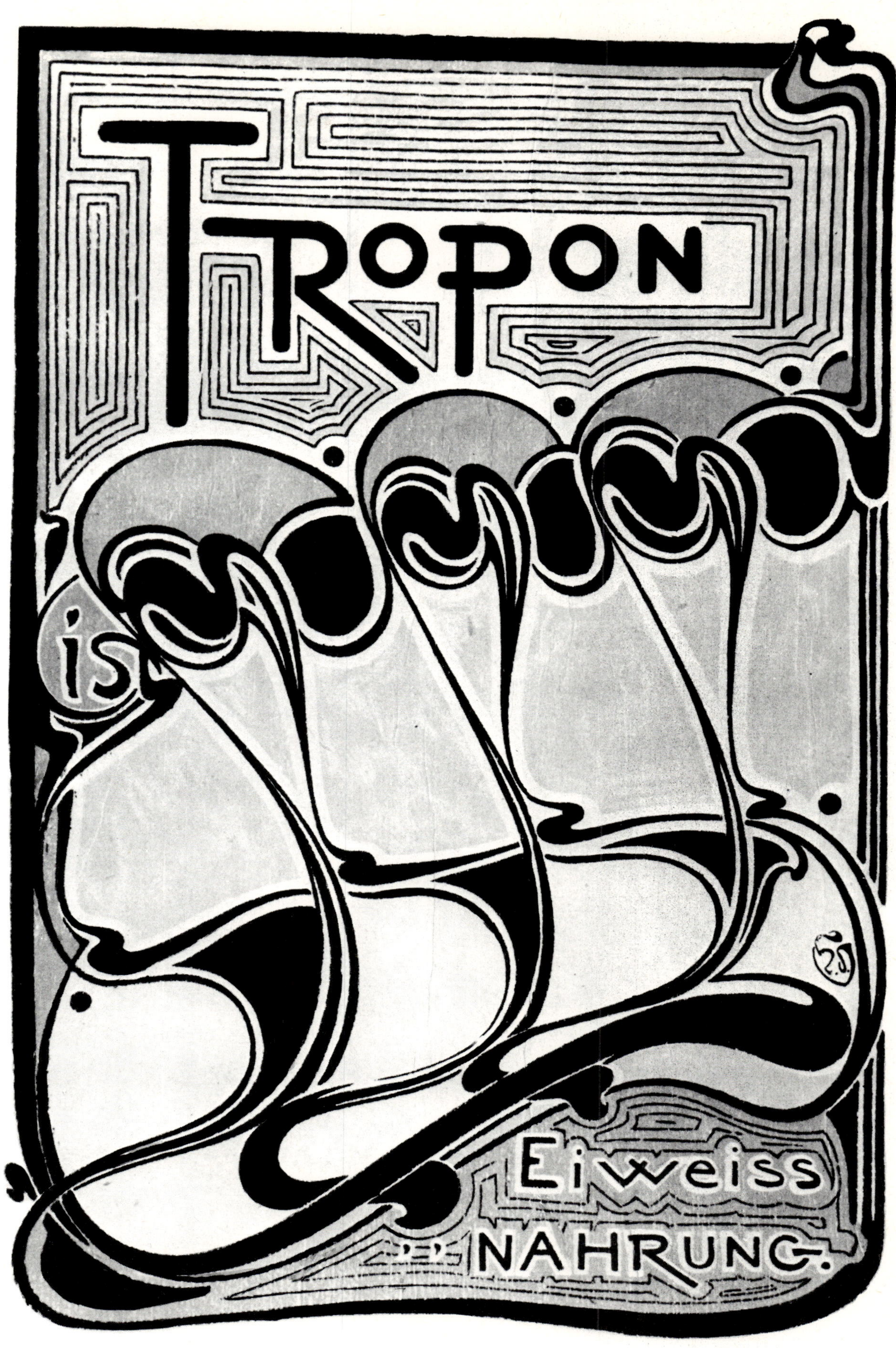


Henry van de Velde
*Tropon* 1897

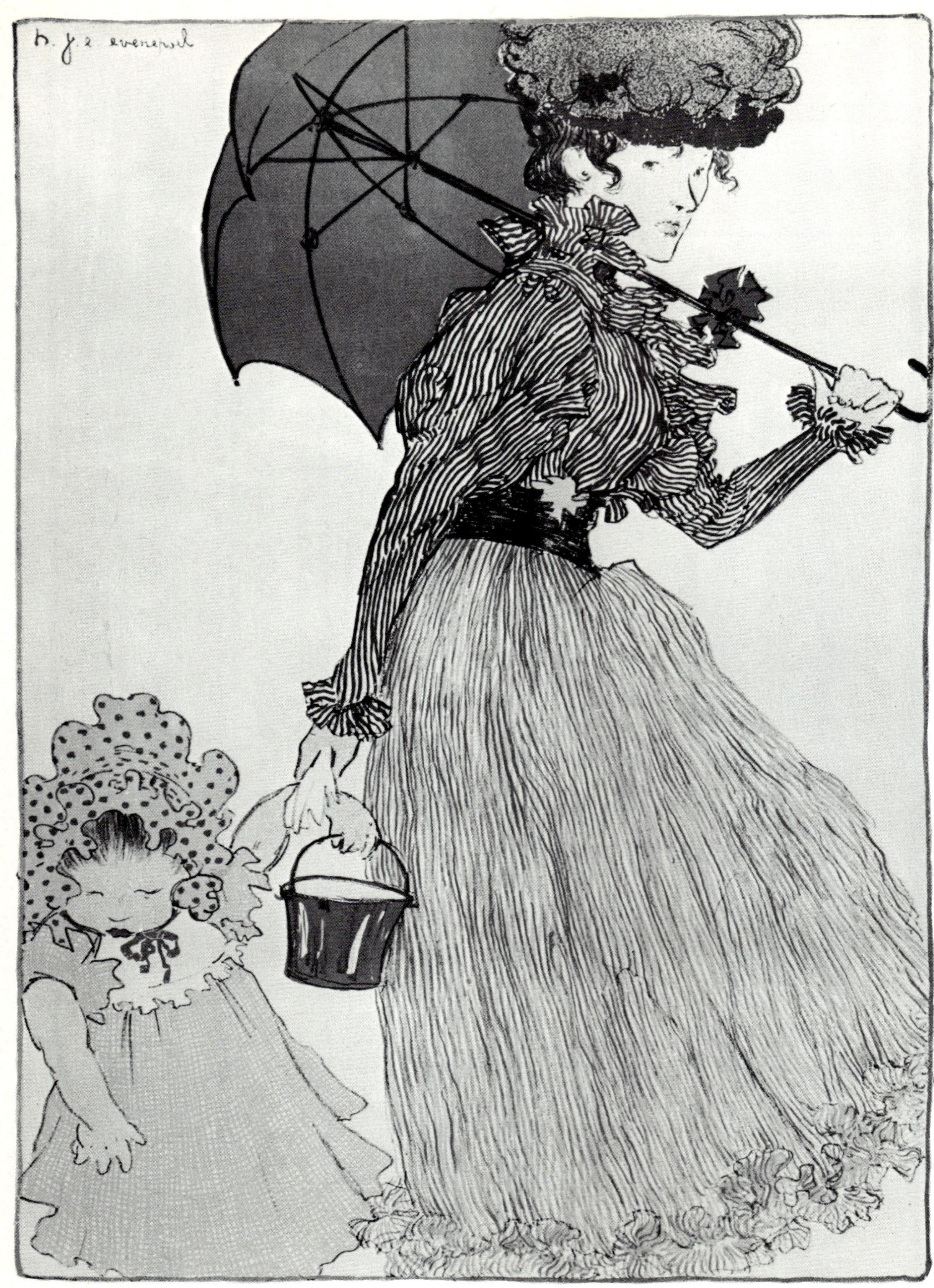


Henri Evenepoel
*L'Estampe moderne: Au Square* 1897

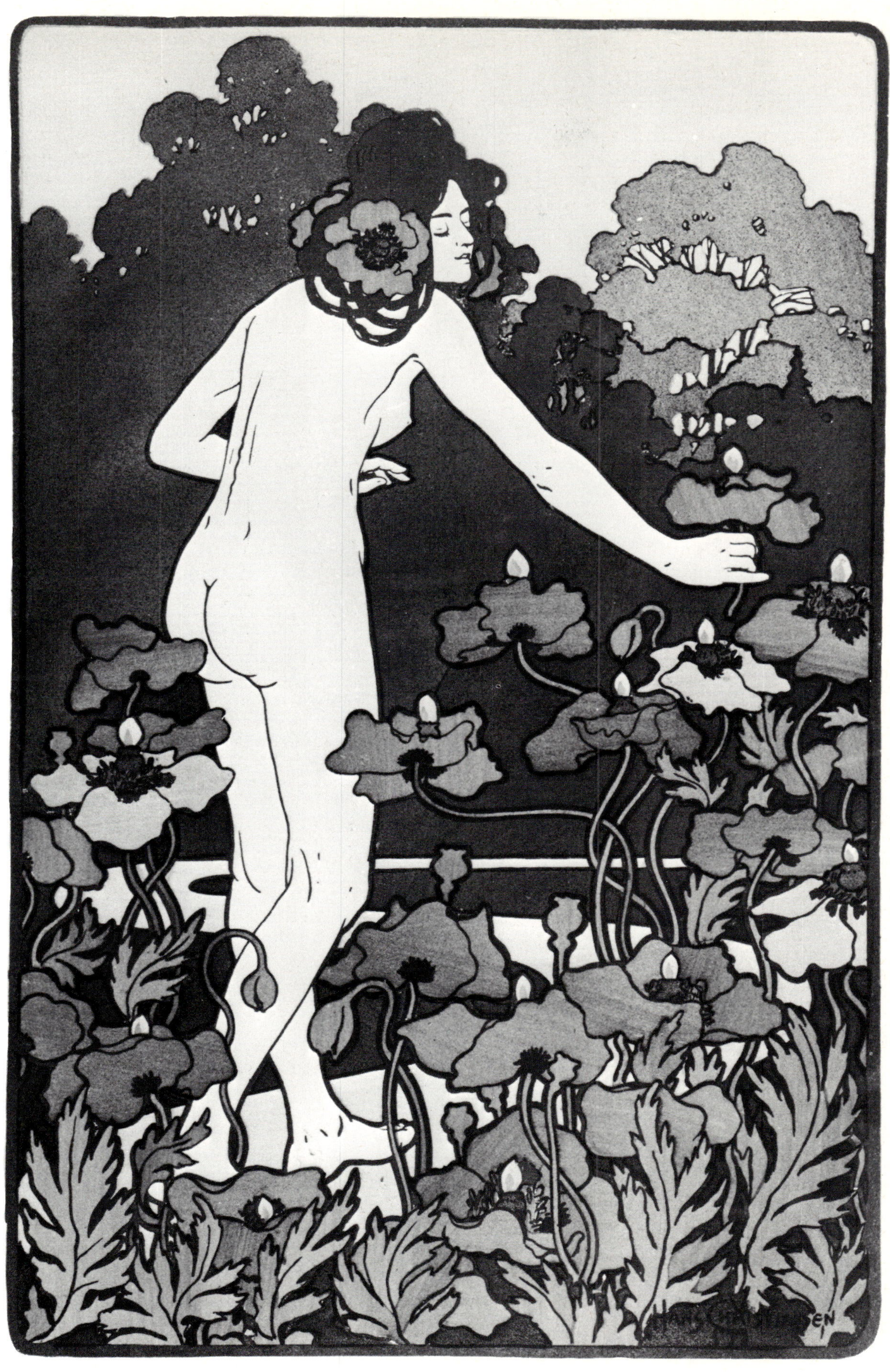

Hans Christiansen
*L'Heure du berger* 1898

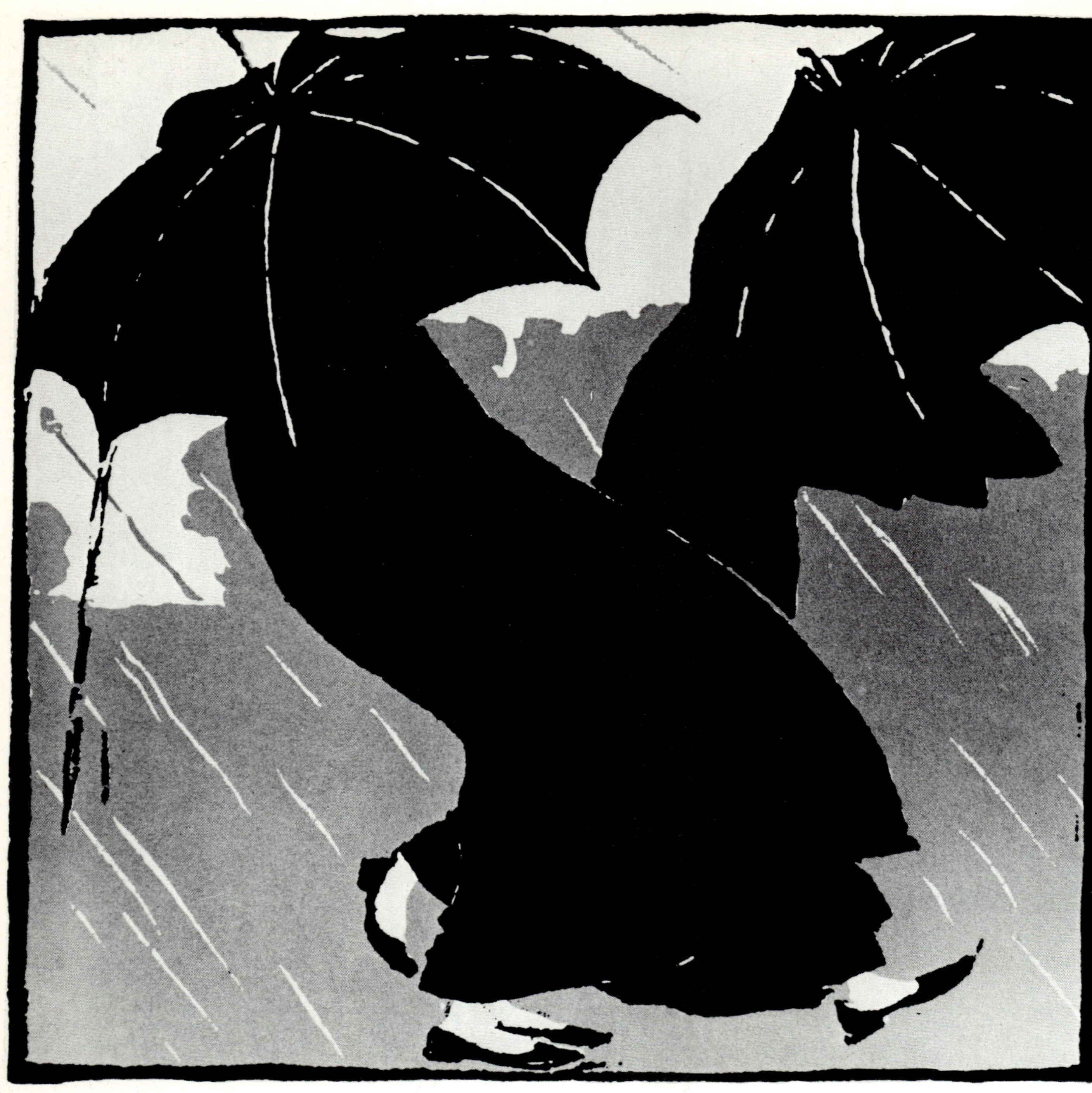

Leopold Stolba
*Ver Sacrum: April*

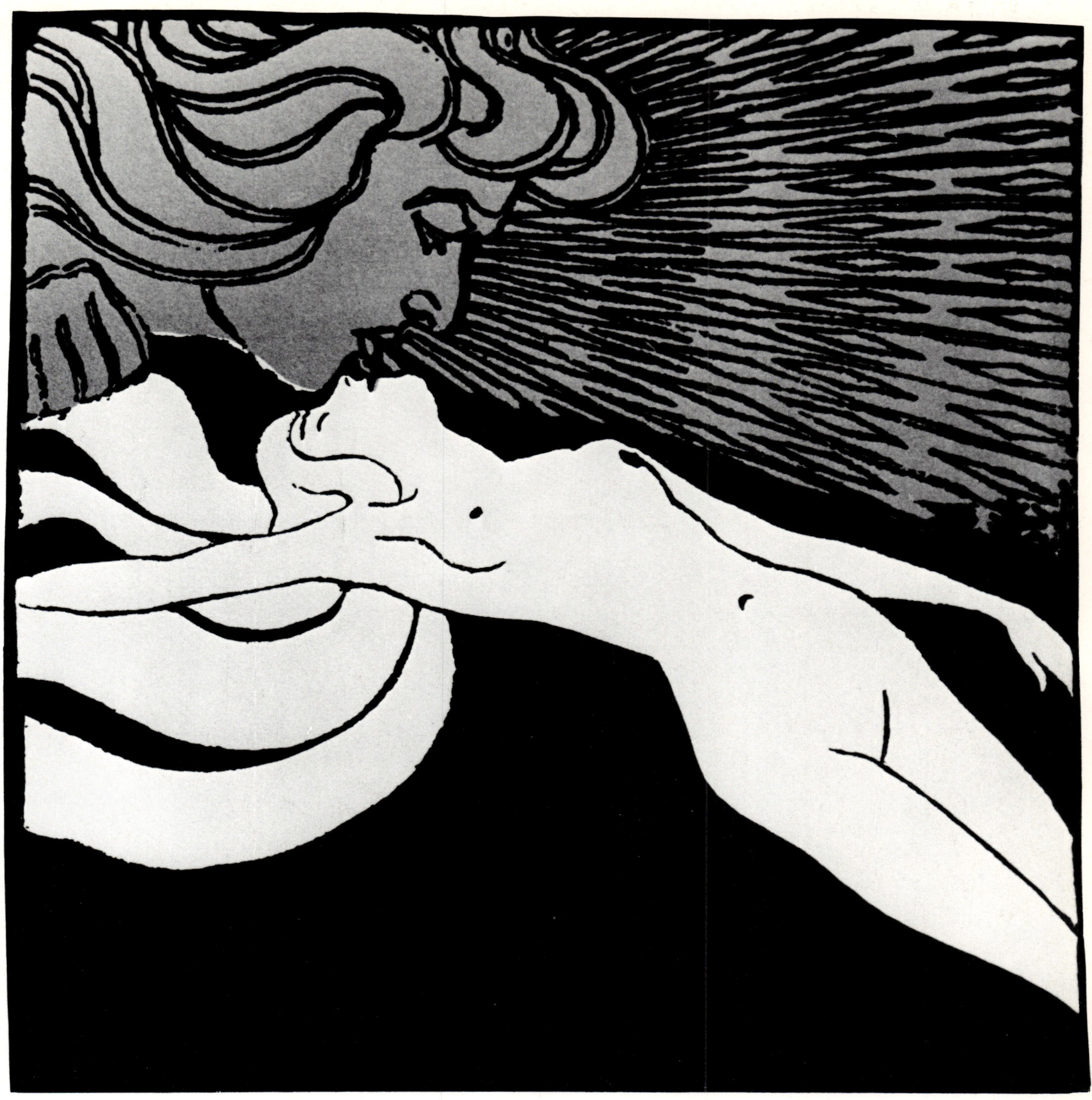

Wilhelm List
*Strahlenküsse* 1903

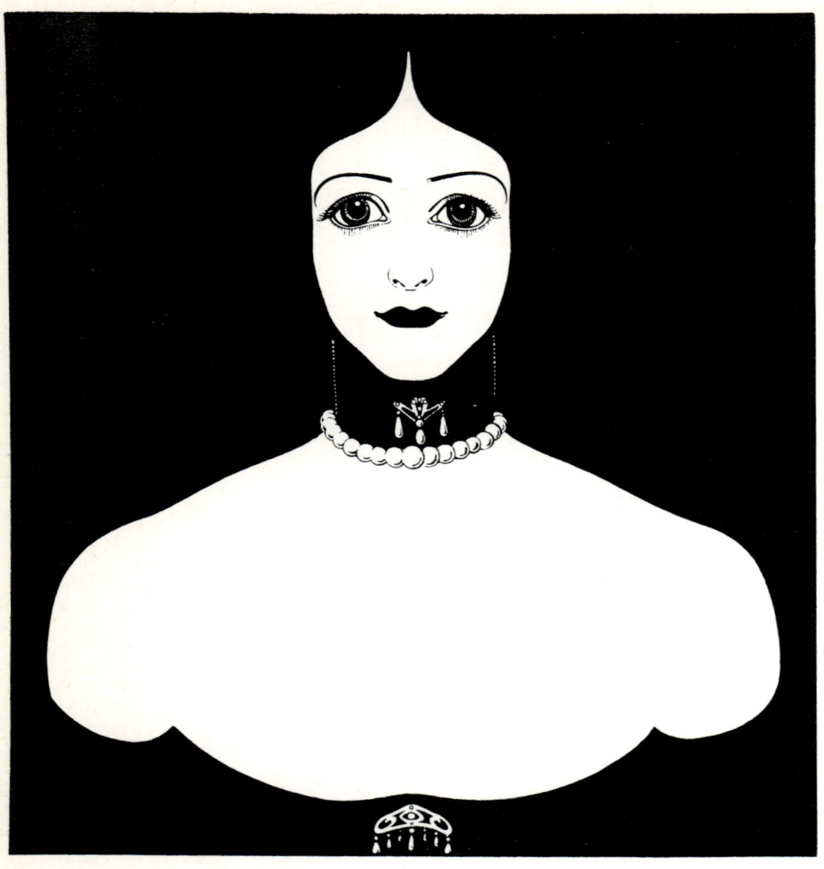

John Jack Vrieslander
*Portrait*

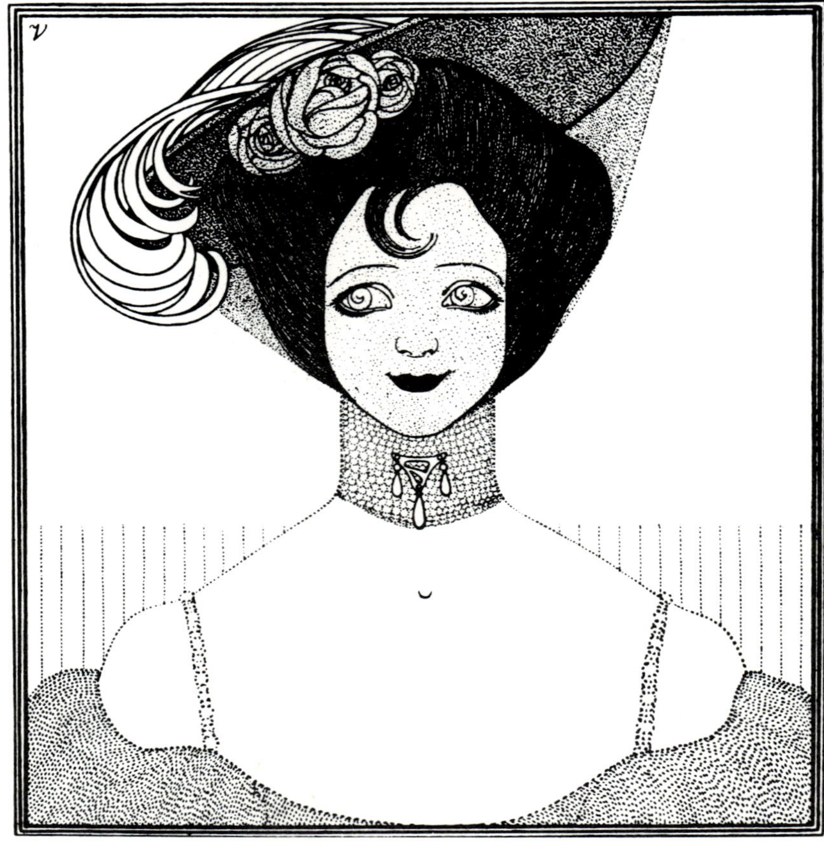

John Jack Vrieslander
*Im Nachtcafe / La Soupeuse*

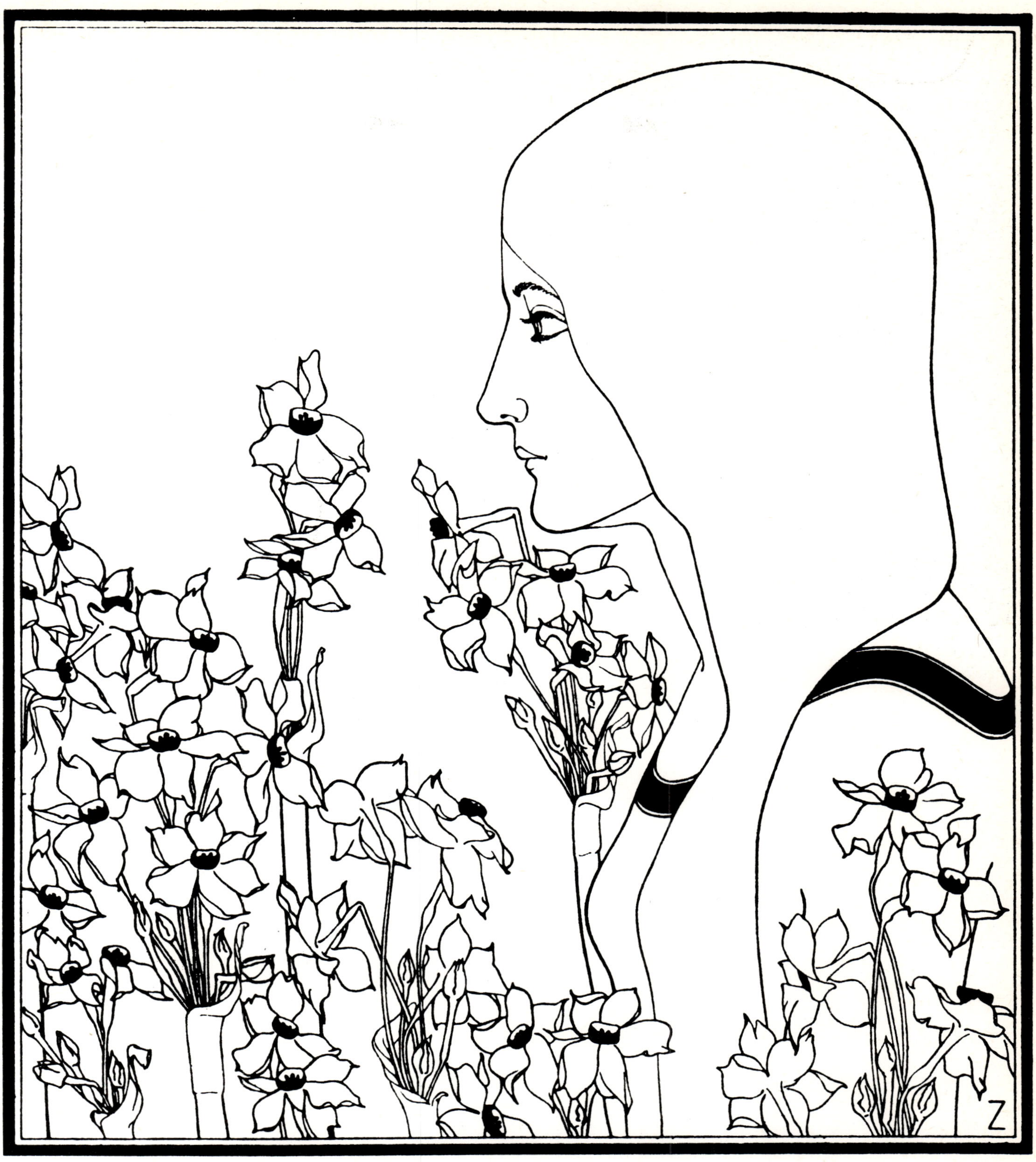

Hans Zarth
*Narcissen / Narcisse*

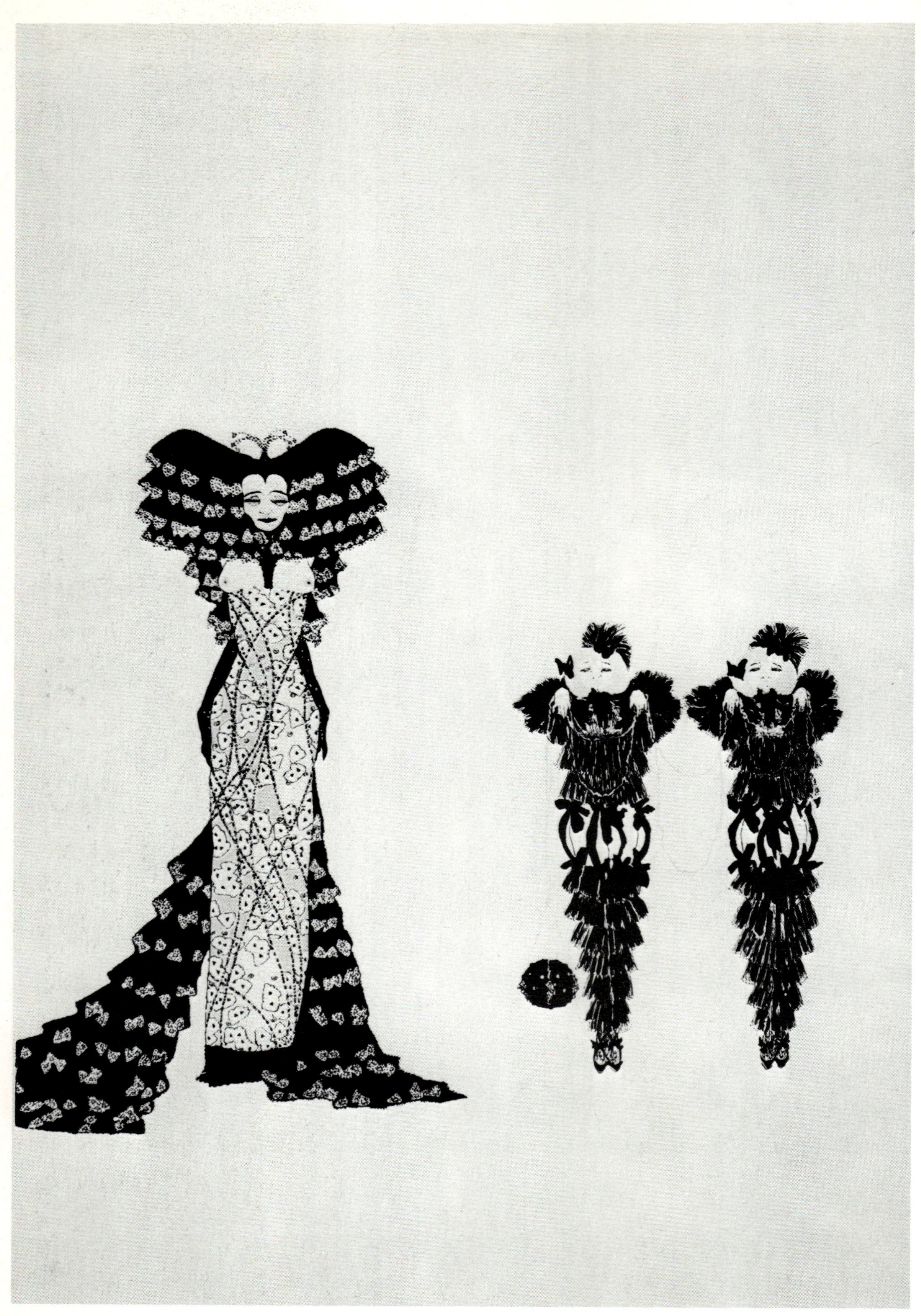

Alastair (Hans Henning, baron Voigt)
*Messalina*

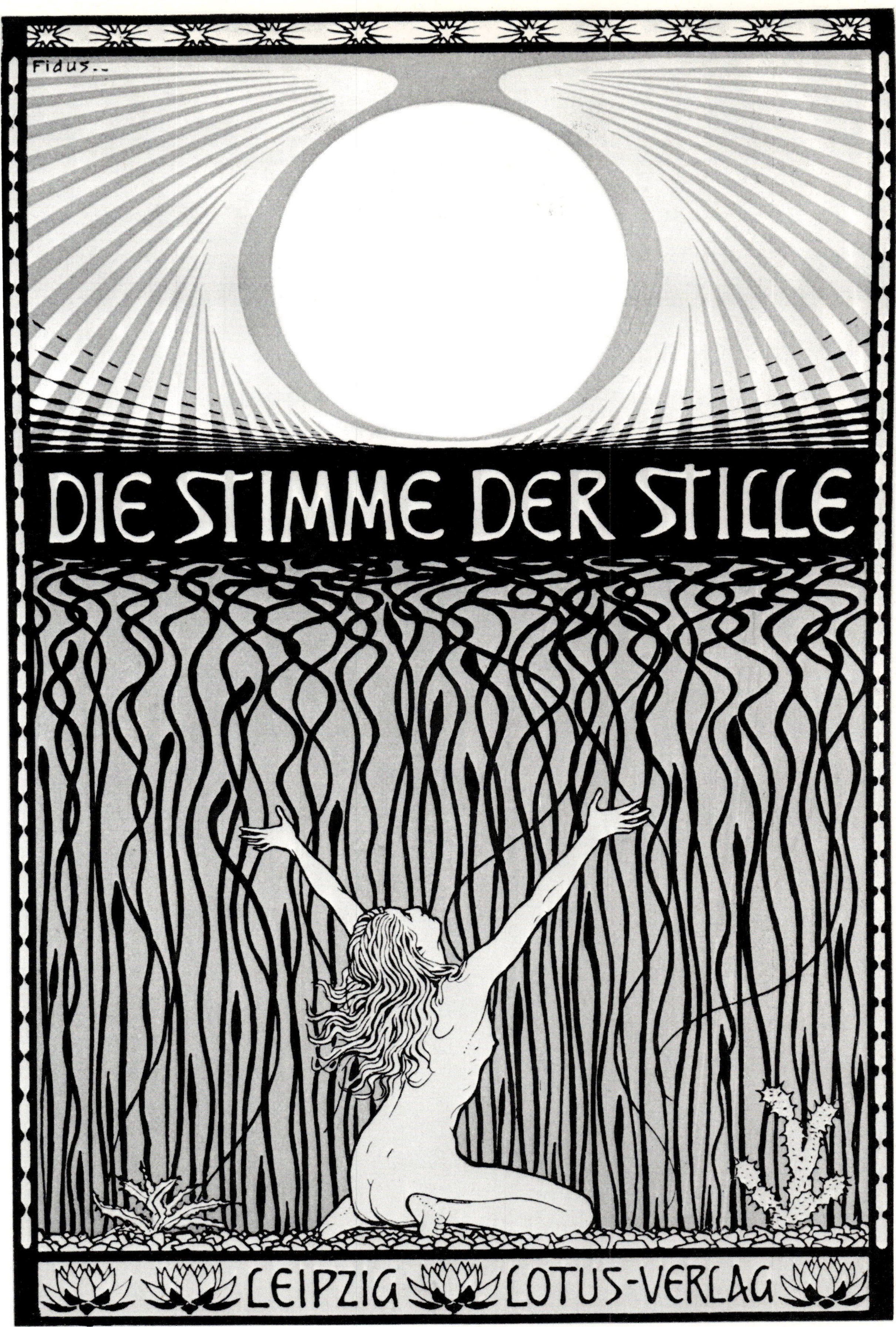


Fidus (Hans Höppener)
*Die Stimme der Stille* 1902

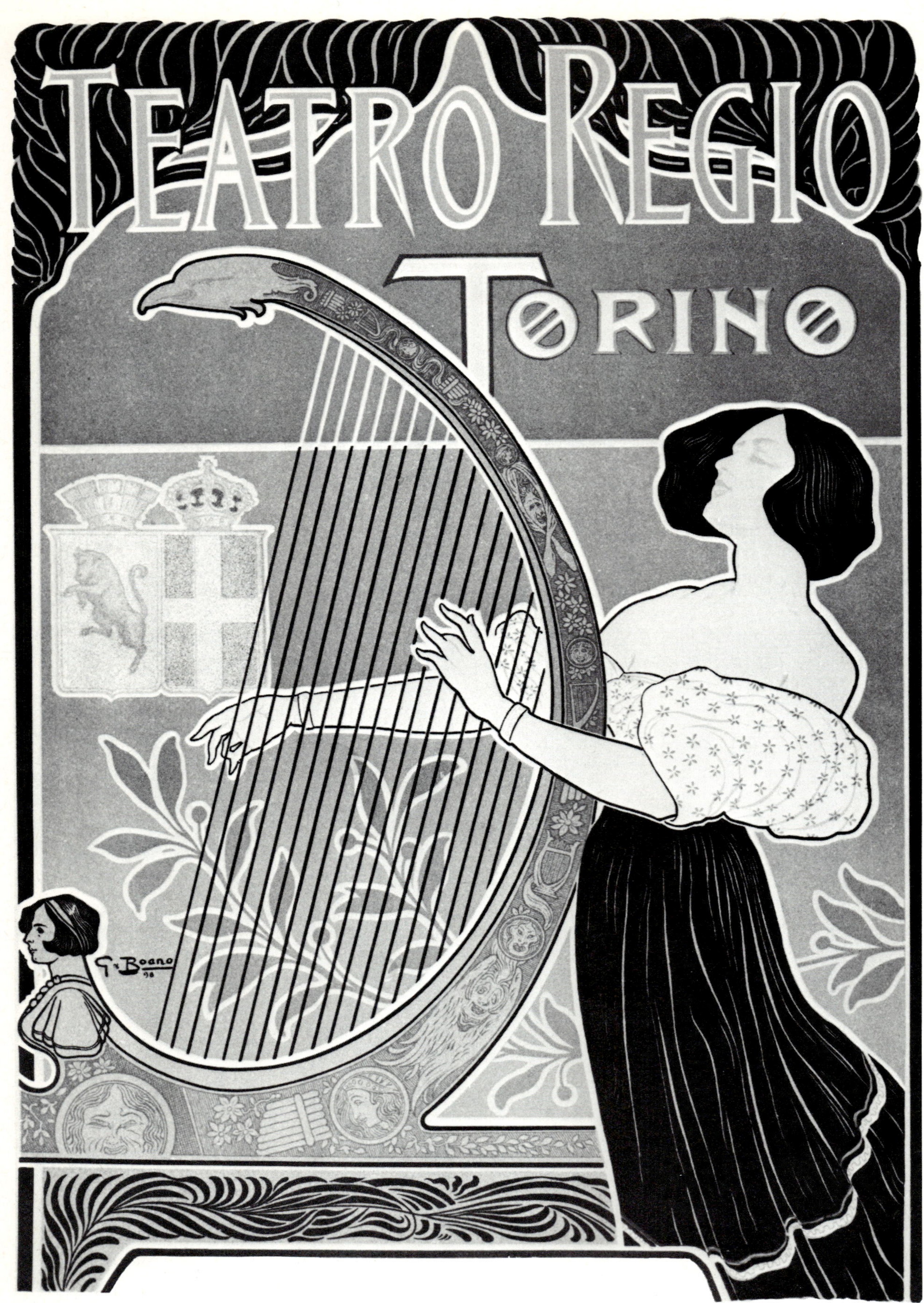


G. Boano
*Teatro Regio Torino* 1898

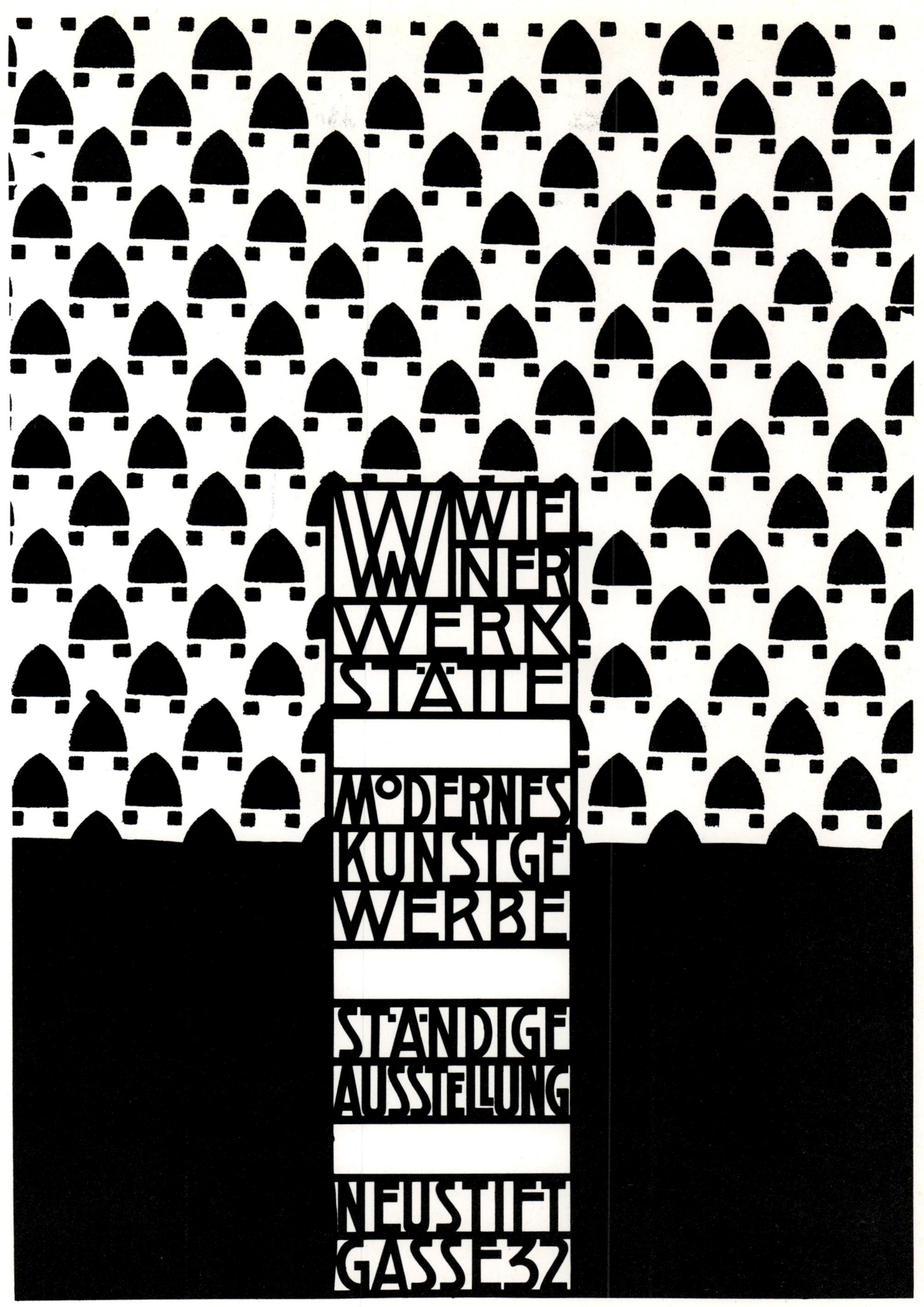


Josef Hoffman
*Wiener Werkstätte* 1905

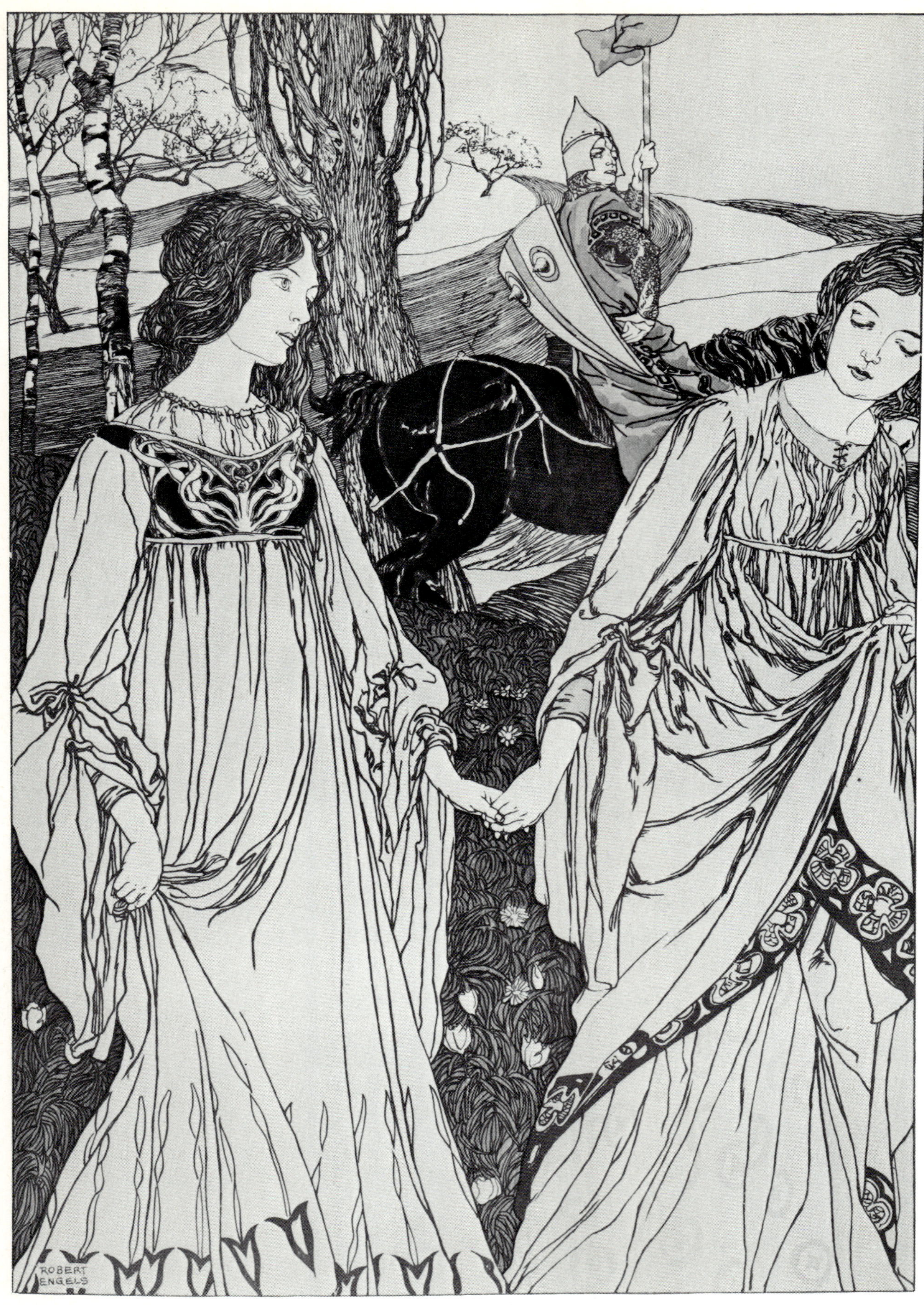


Robert Engels
*L'Estampe moderne: Le Passant* 1898

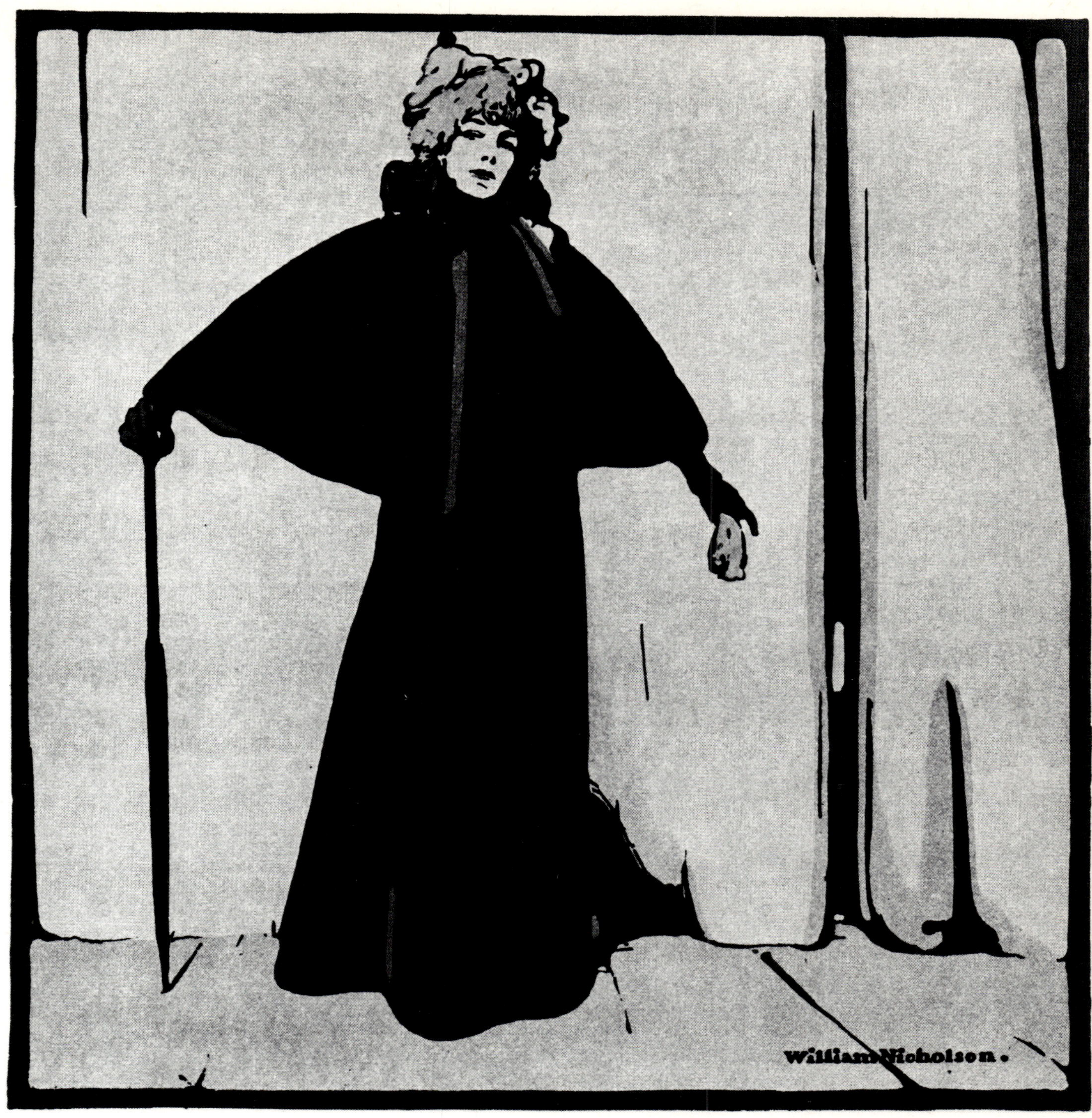


William Nicholson
*Sarah Bernhardt* 1899

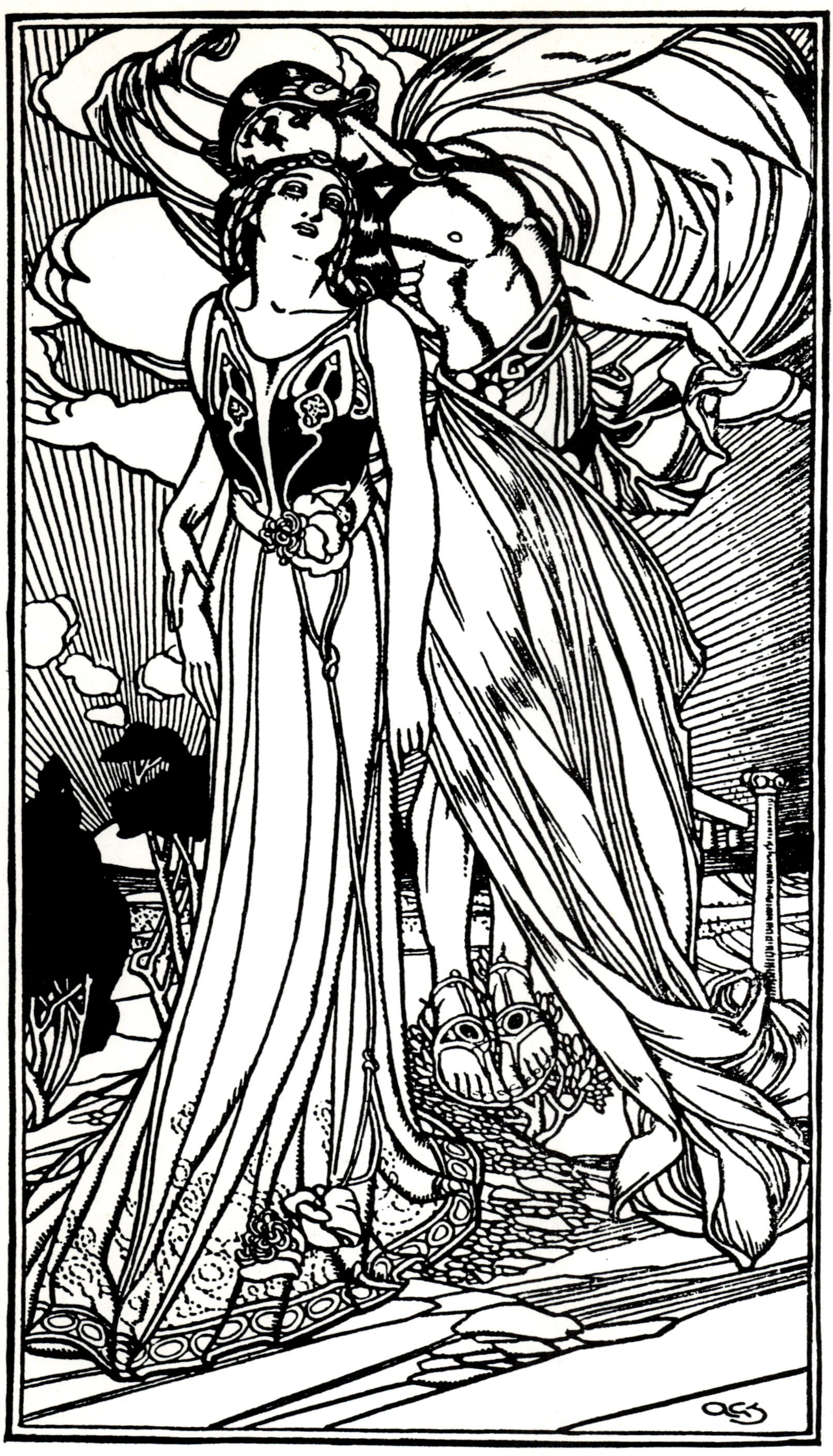

A. Garth Jones
John Milton: *Zephyr & Aurora*

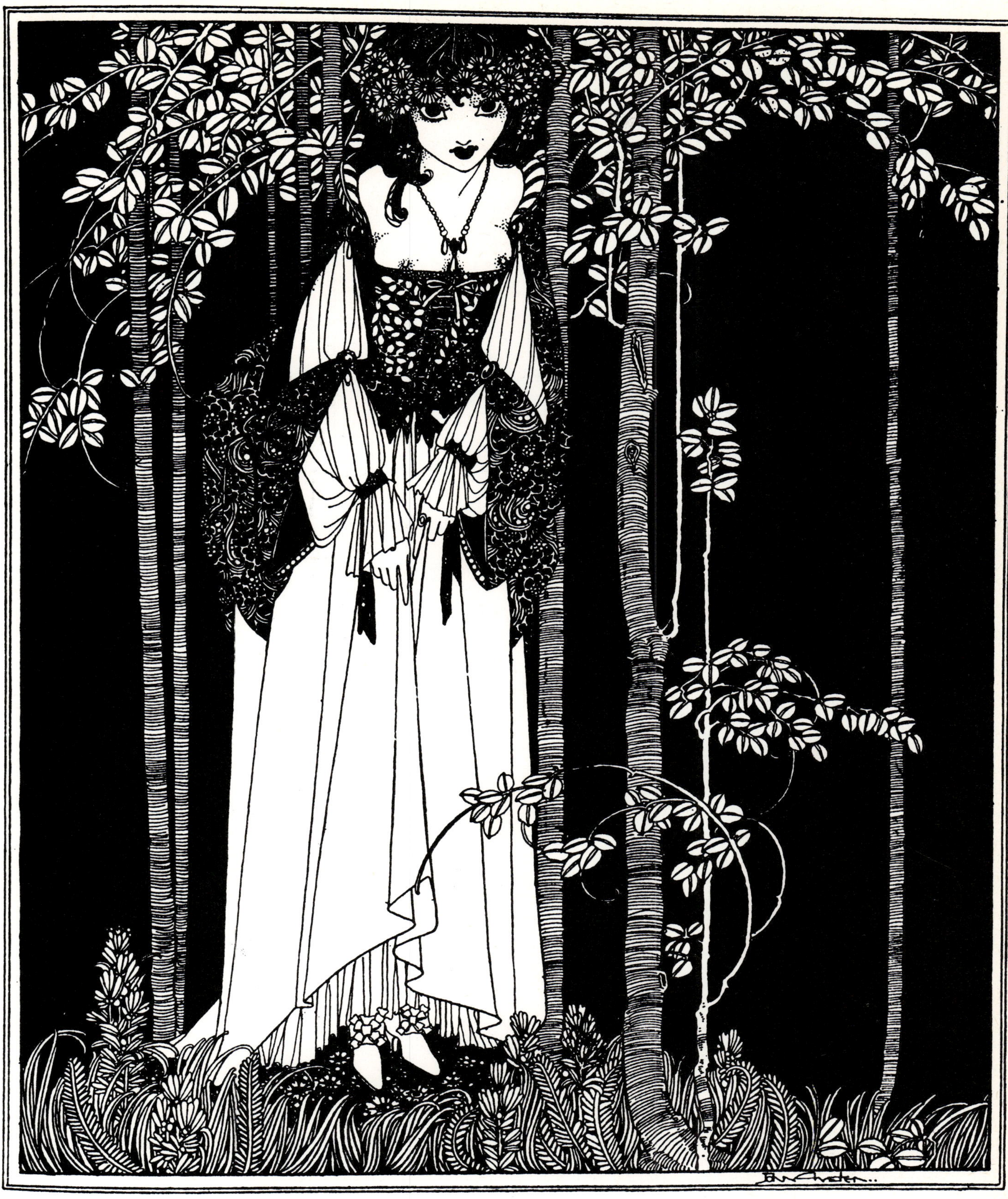

John Austen
*Hamlet: Ophelia*

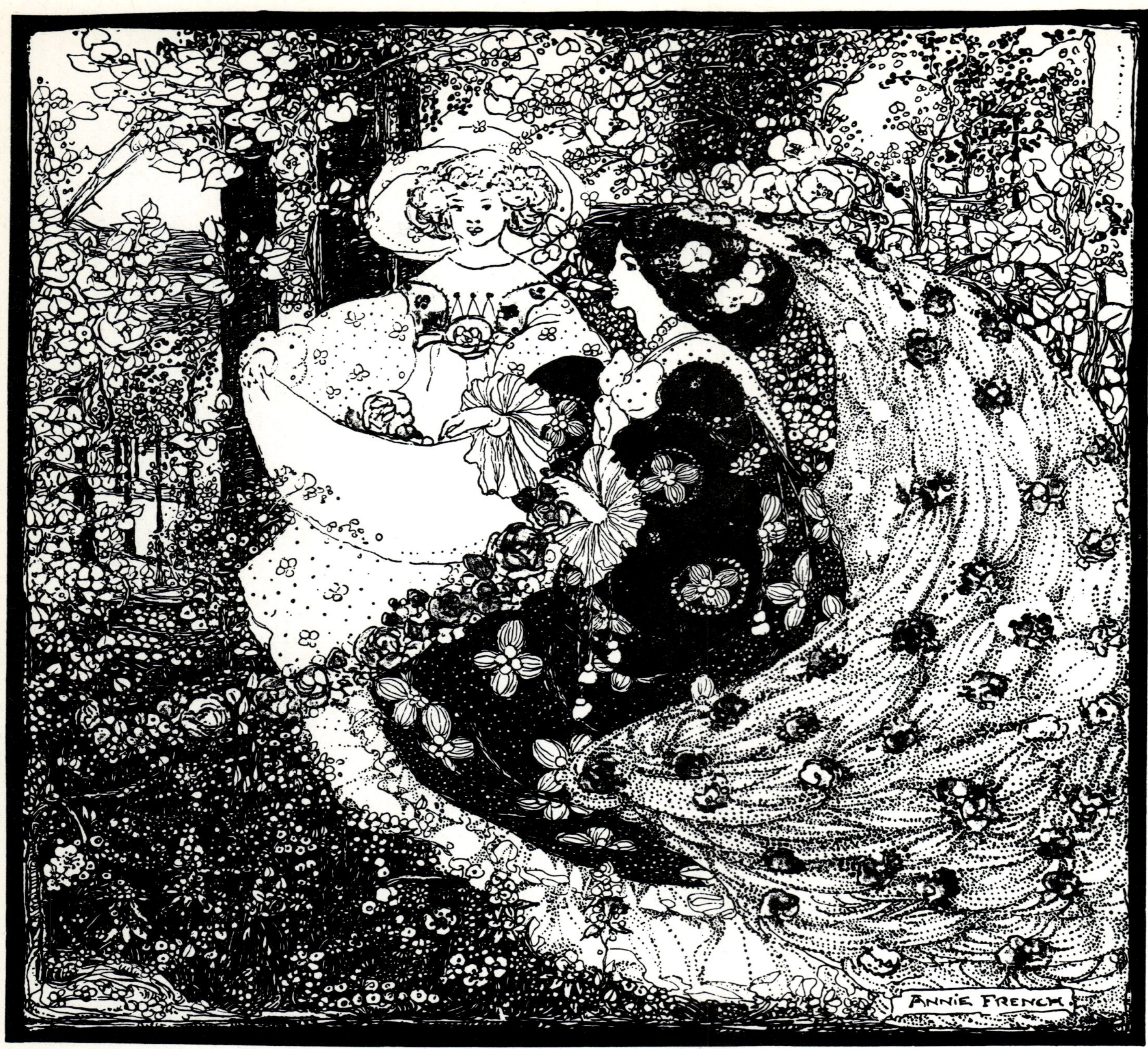


Annie French
*The Garland* *c* 1906

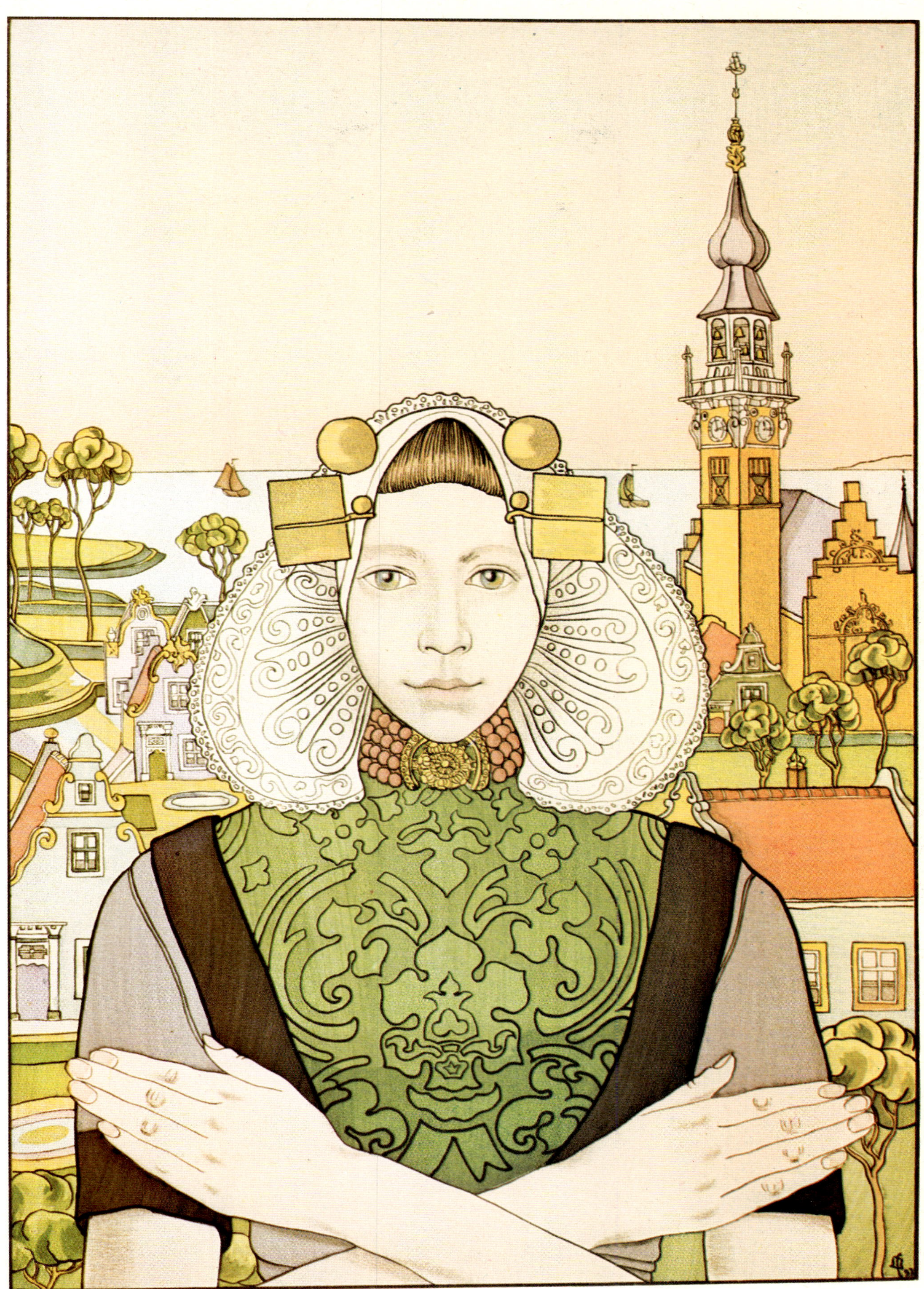

Franz M. Melchers
*L'Estampe moderne: La Phalène des îles de la mer* 1897

DÜSSELDORF.

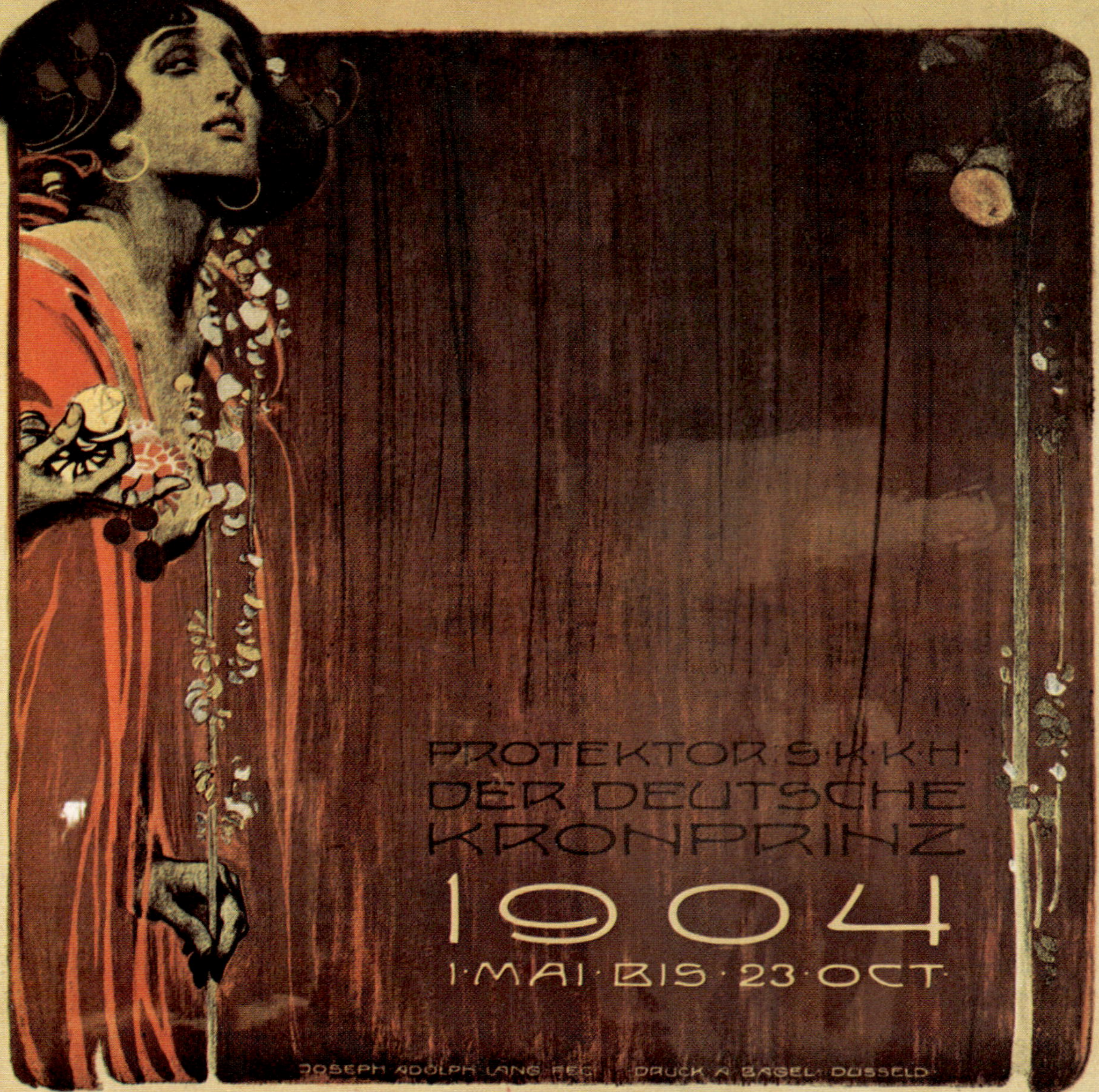


INTERNATIONALE
KUNST UND GARTENBAU
AUSSTELLUNG

Joseph Adolph Lang
*Dusseldorf Internationale Kunst und Gartenbau Austellung* 1904

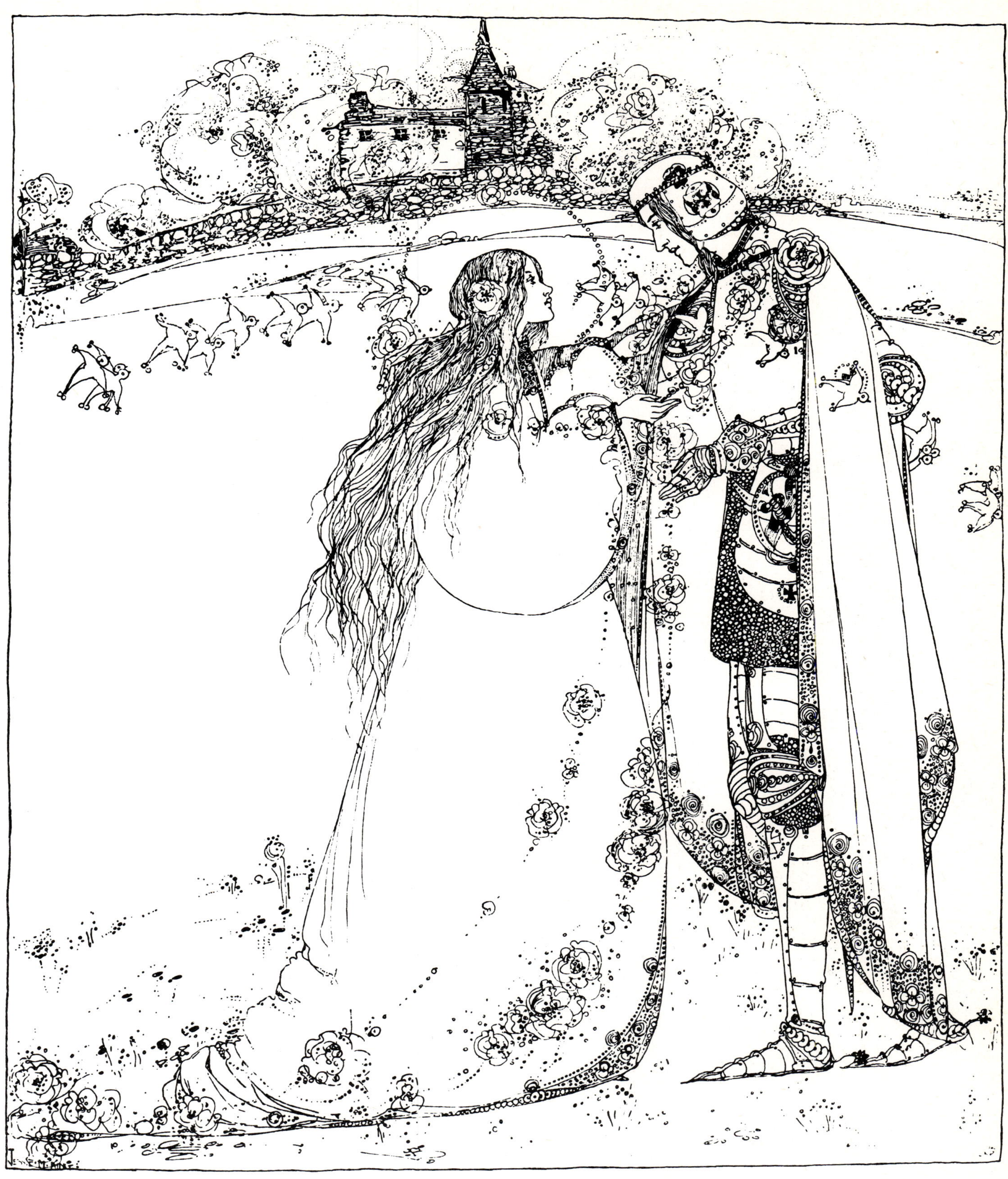

Jessie M. King
*The Little Princess c* 1902

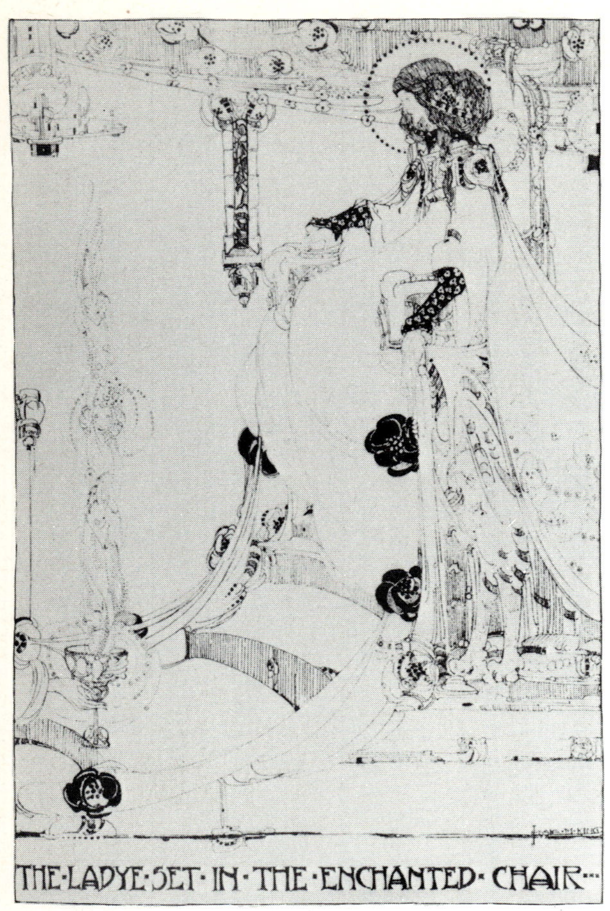


Jessie M. King
John Milton – *Comus: A Masque*

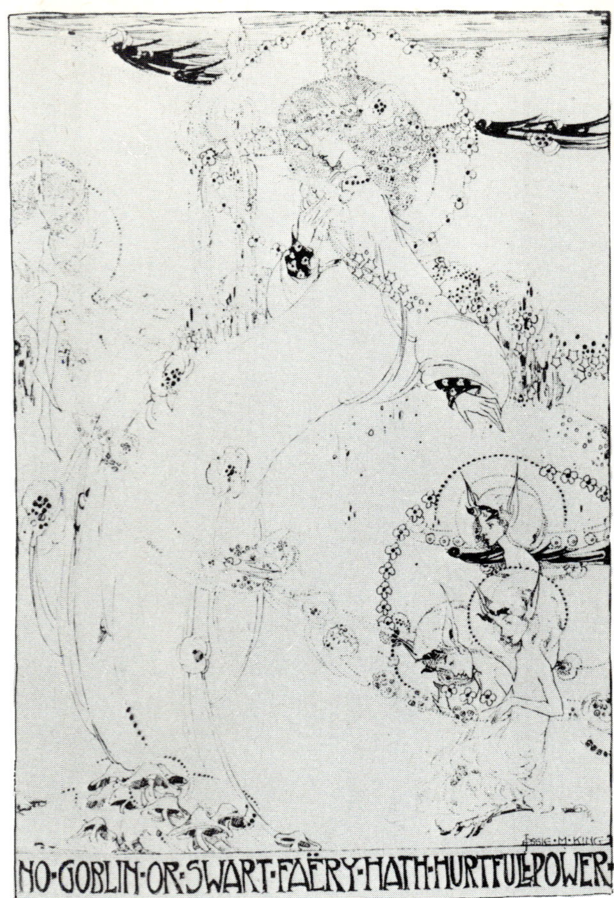


Jessie M. King
John Milton – *Comus: A Masque*

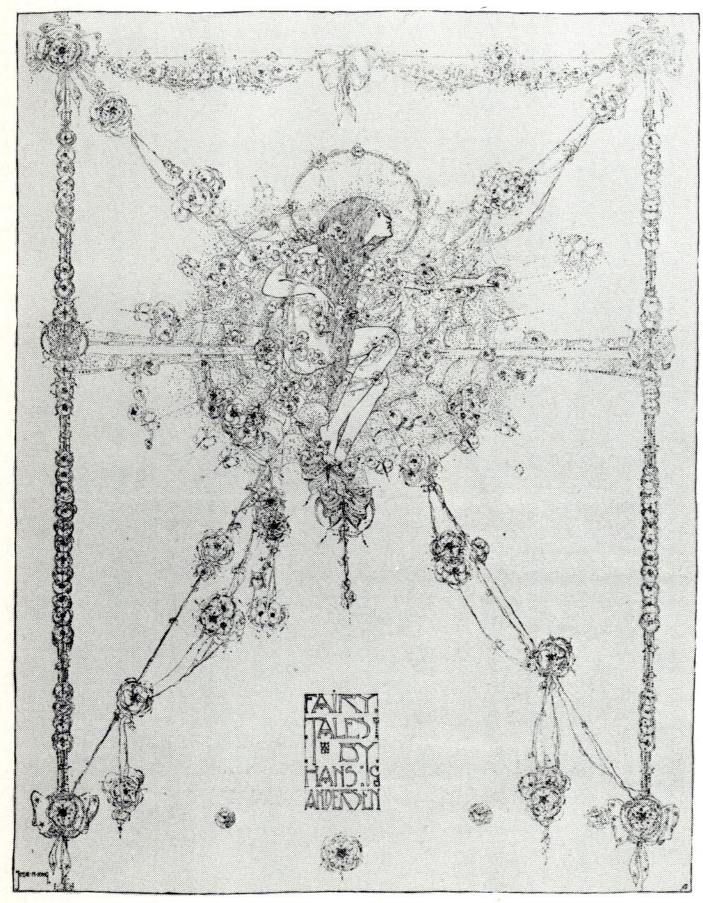


Jessie M. King
*Hans Christian Andersen c* 1902

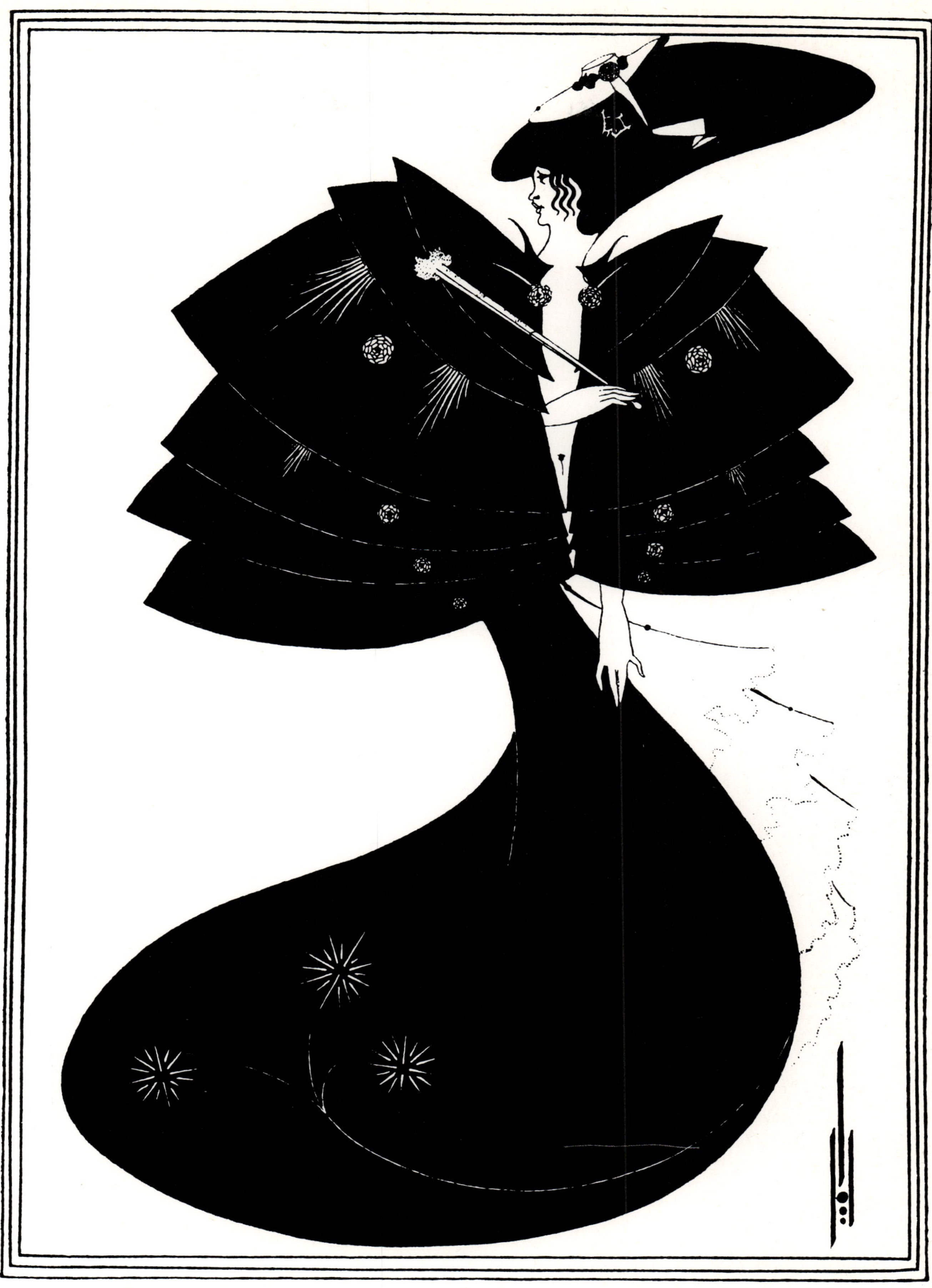

Aubrey Beardsley
*Salomé: The Black Cape* 1894

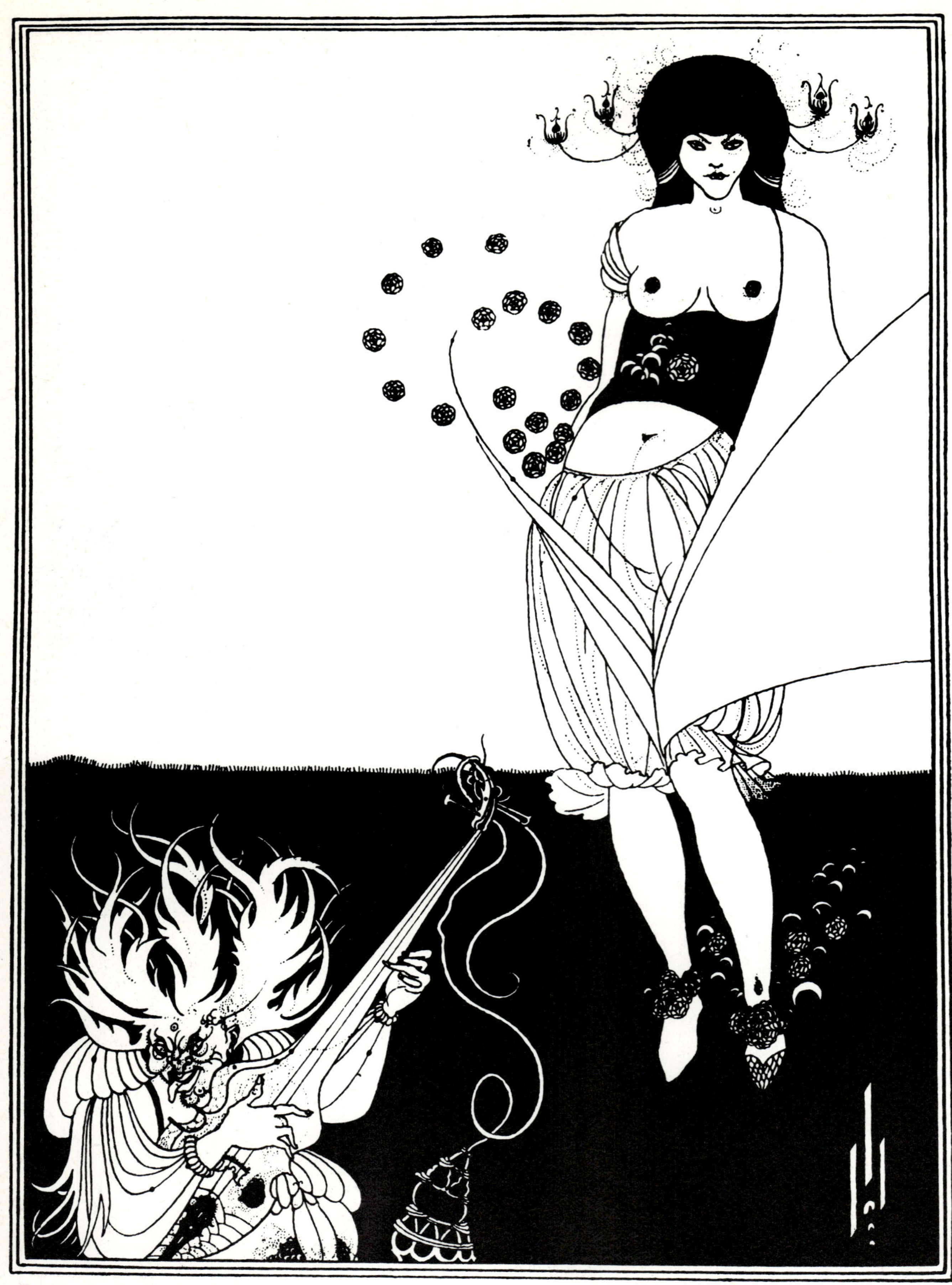

Aubrey Beardsley
*Salomé: The Stomach Dance* 1894

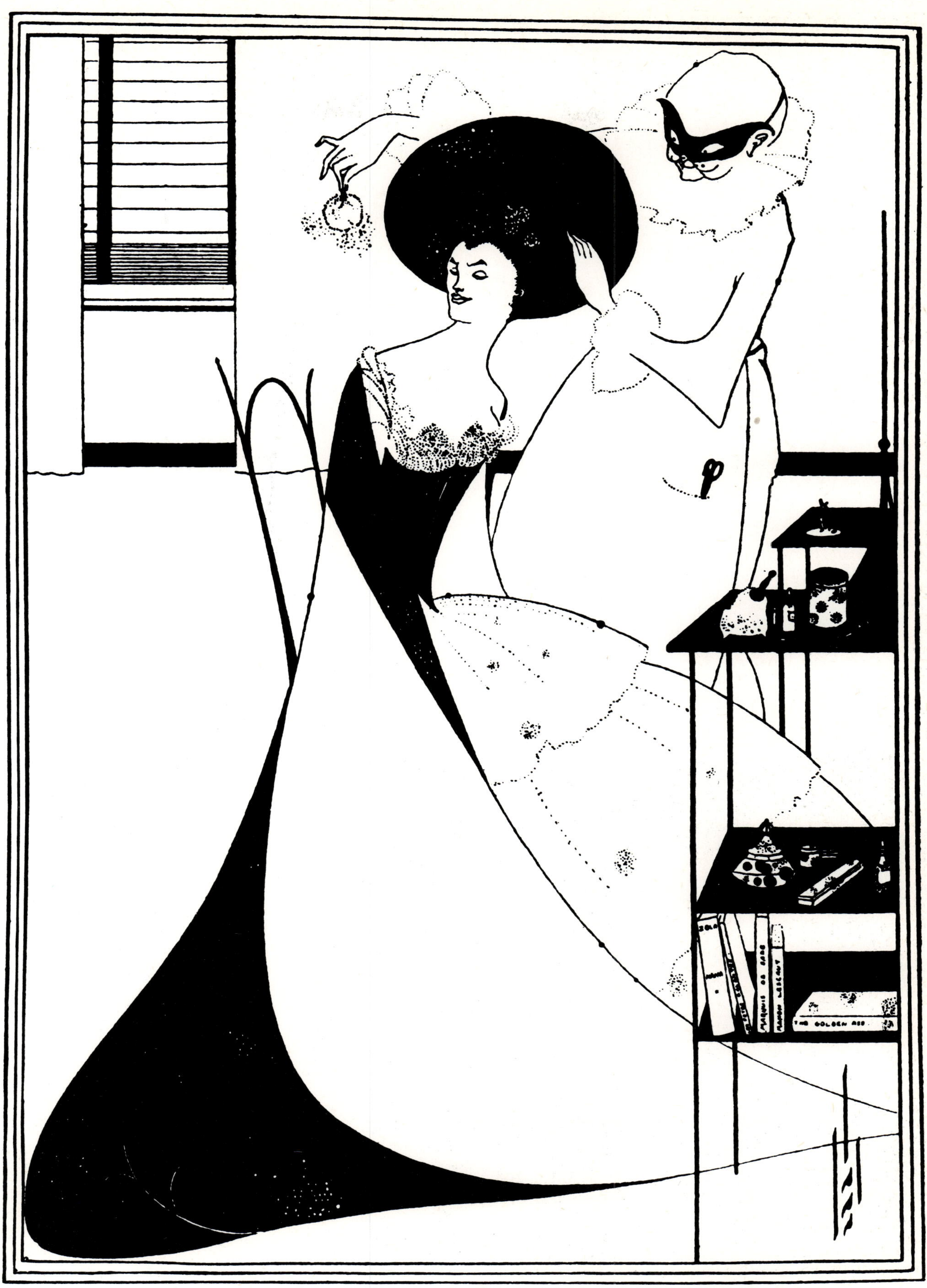


Aubrey Beardsley
*Salomé: The Toilet of Salomé* 1894

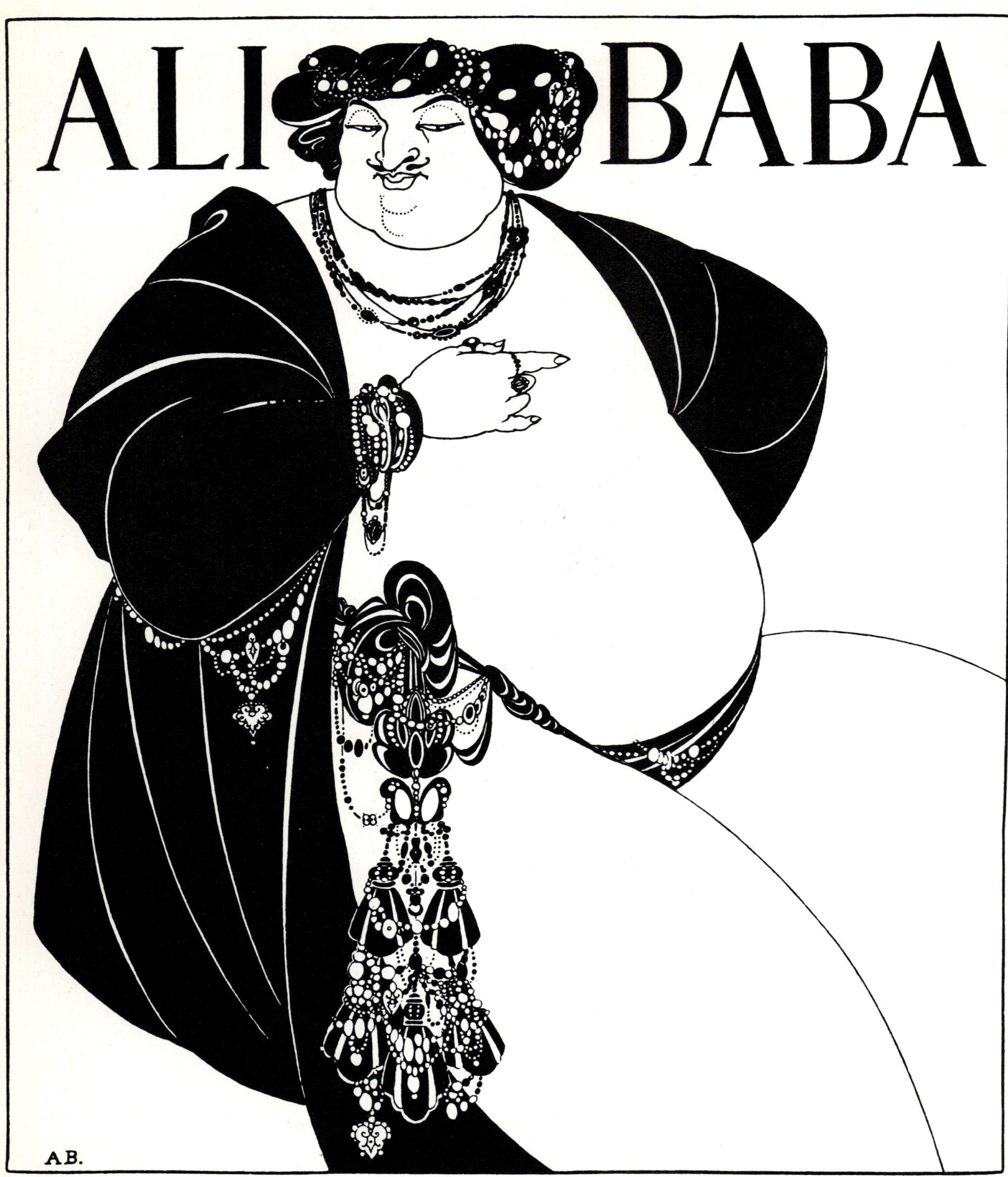


Aubrey Beardsley
*The Forty Thieves: Ali Baba*

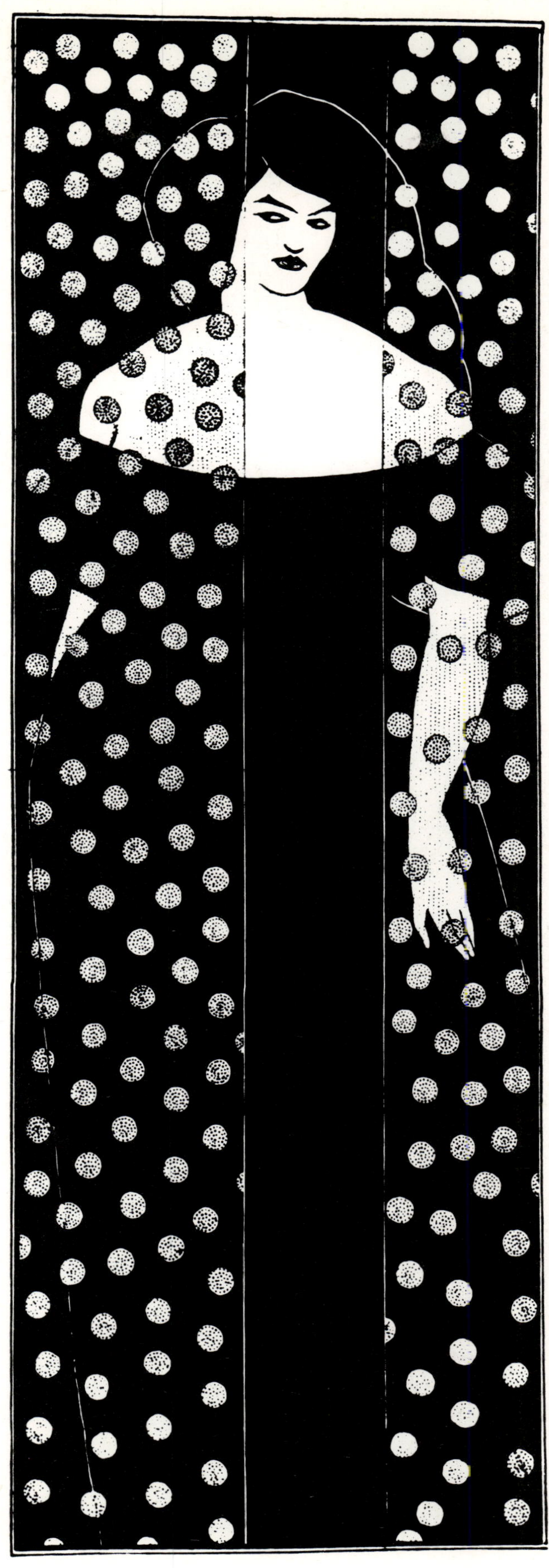

Aubrey Beardsley
*A Comedy of Sighs* 1894

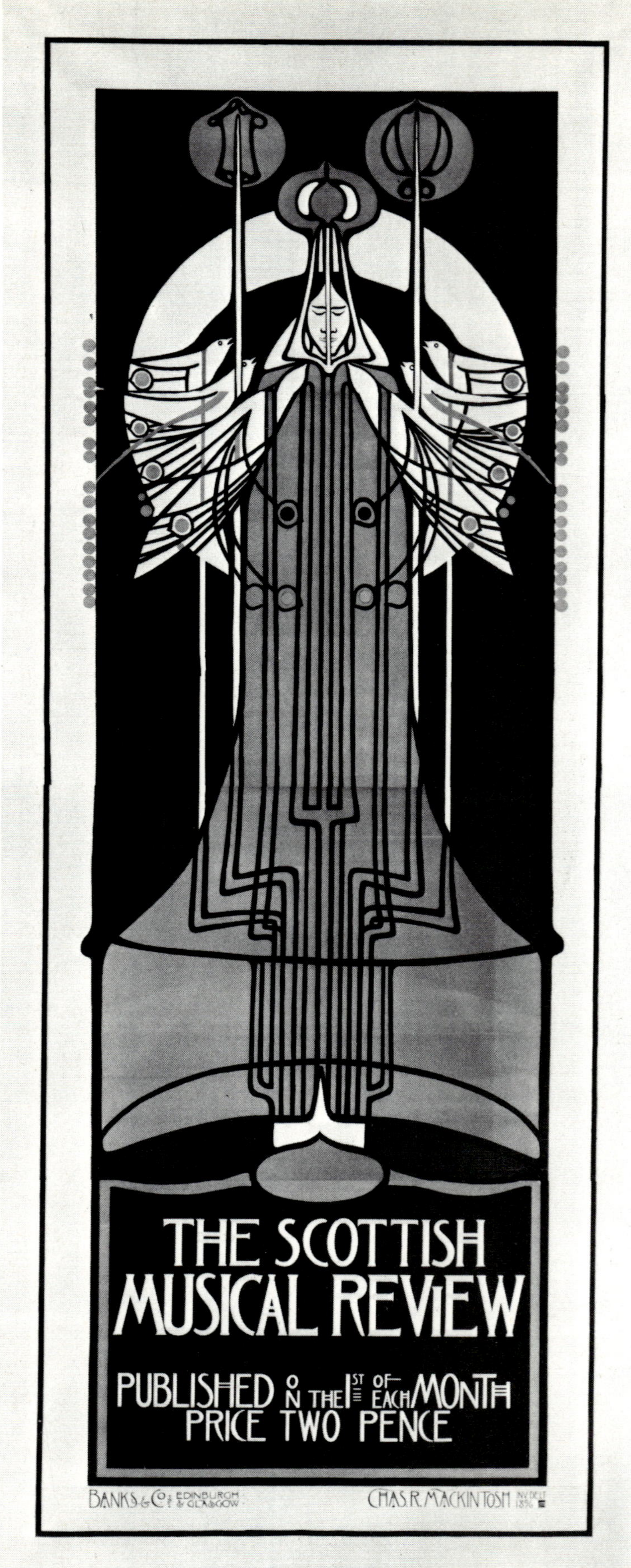


Charles Rennie Mackintosh
*Scottish Musical Review* 1896

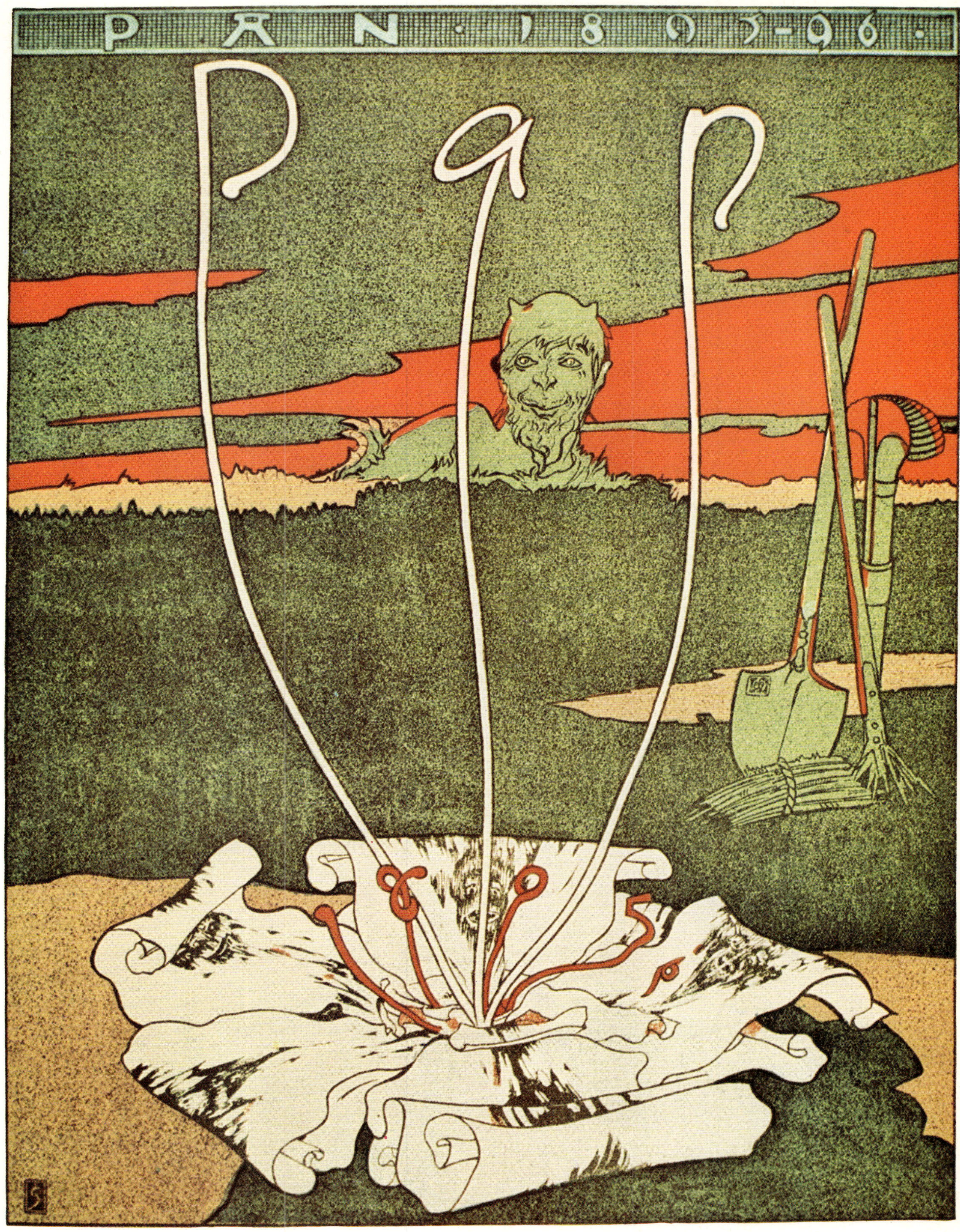


Josef Sattler
*Pan* 1895

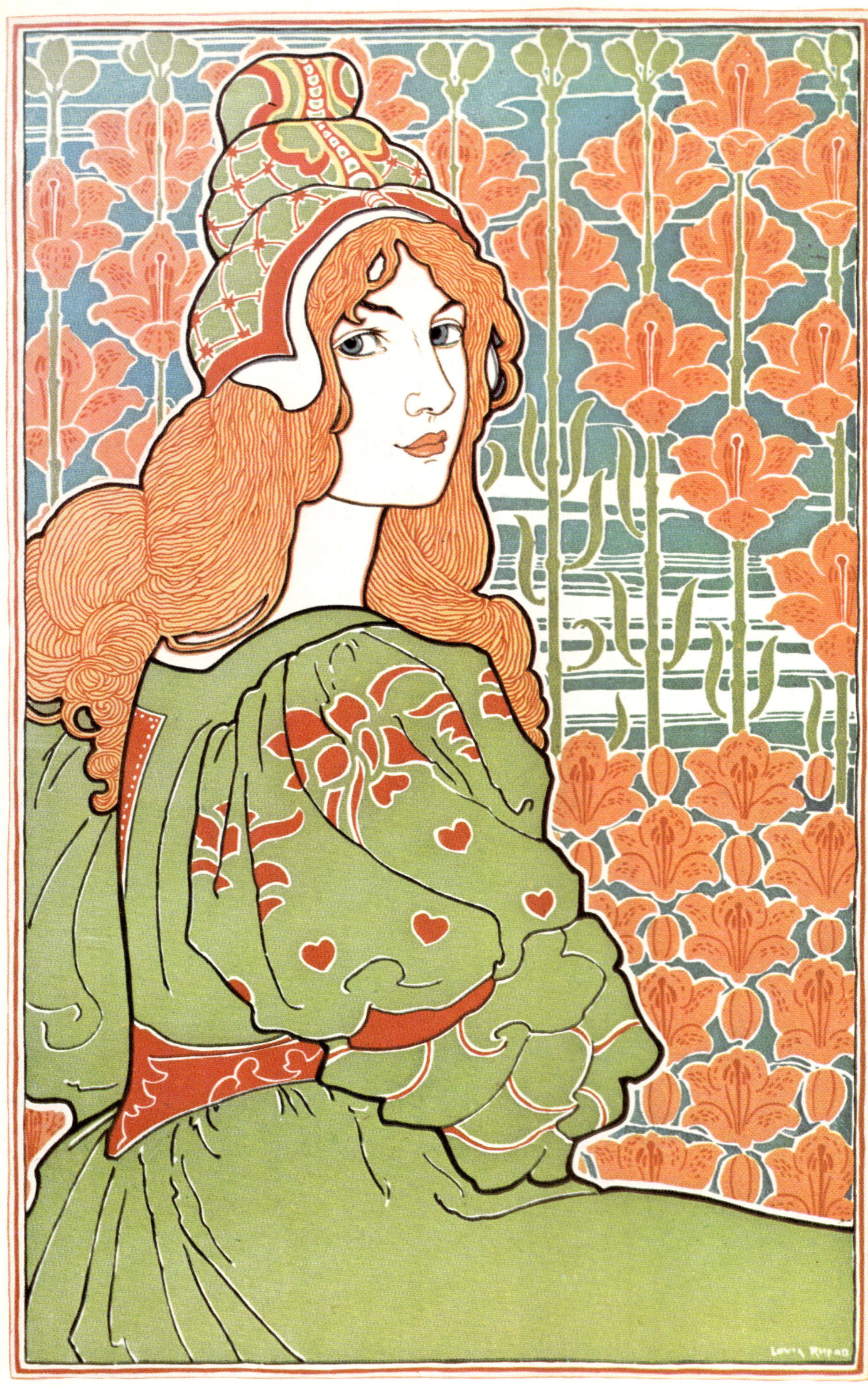

Louis Rhead
*L'Estampe moderne: Jane* 1898

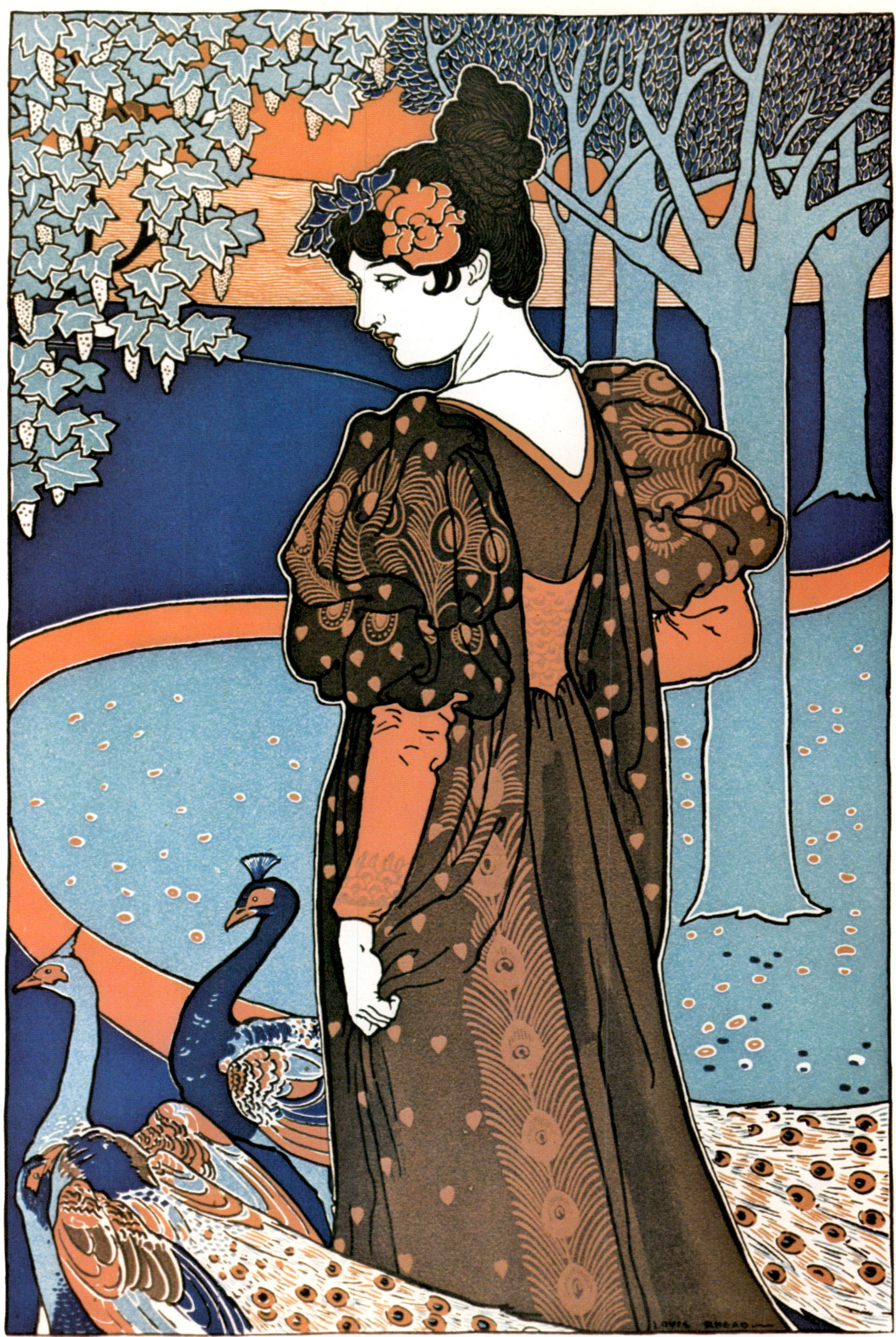


Louis Rhead
*L'Estampe moderne: La Femme au paon* 1897

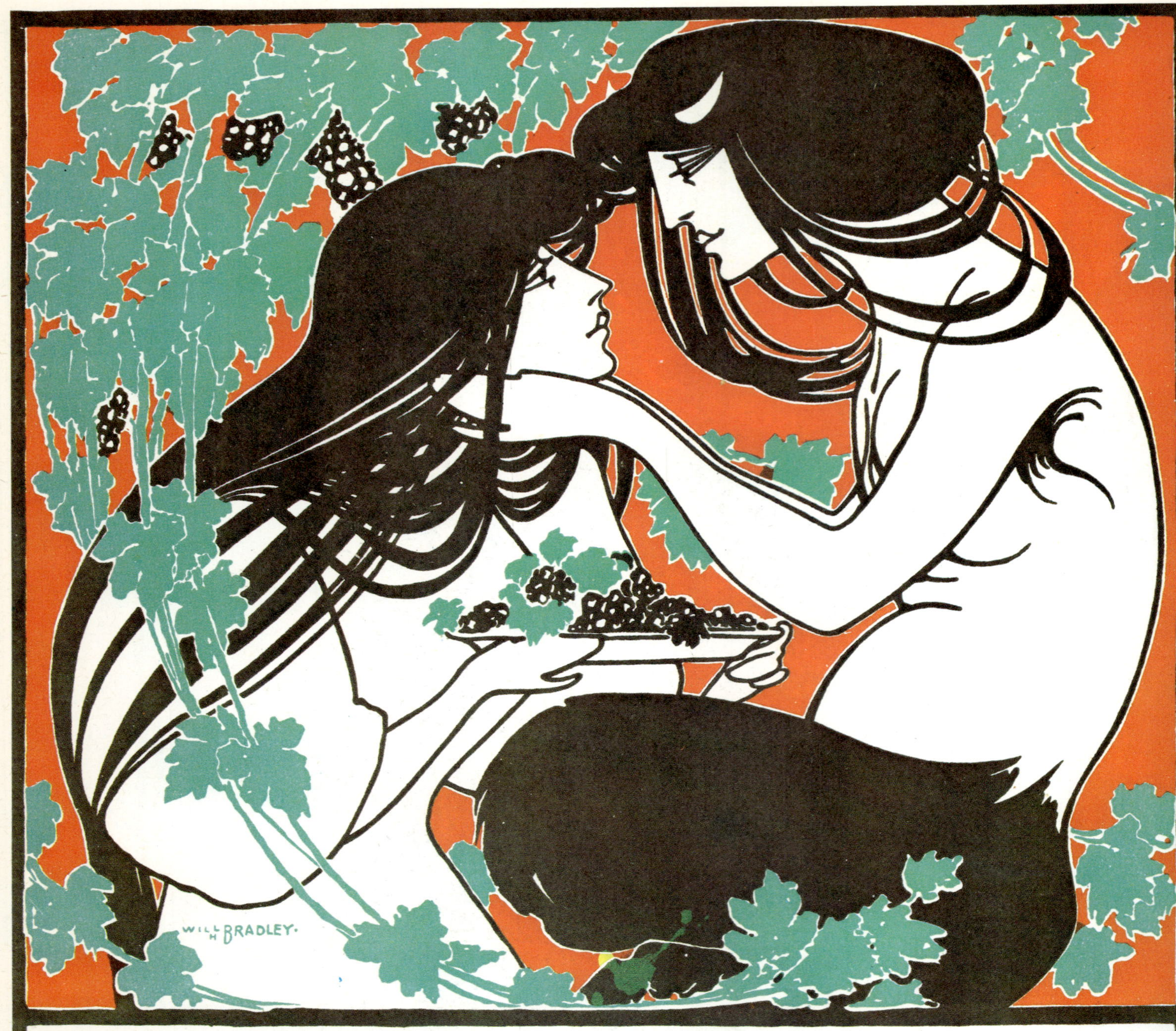


Will H. Bradley
*When Hearts are Trumps* 1894

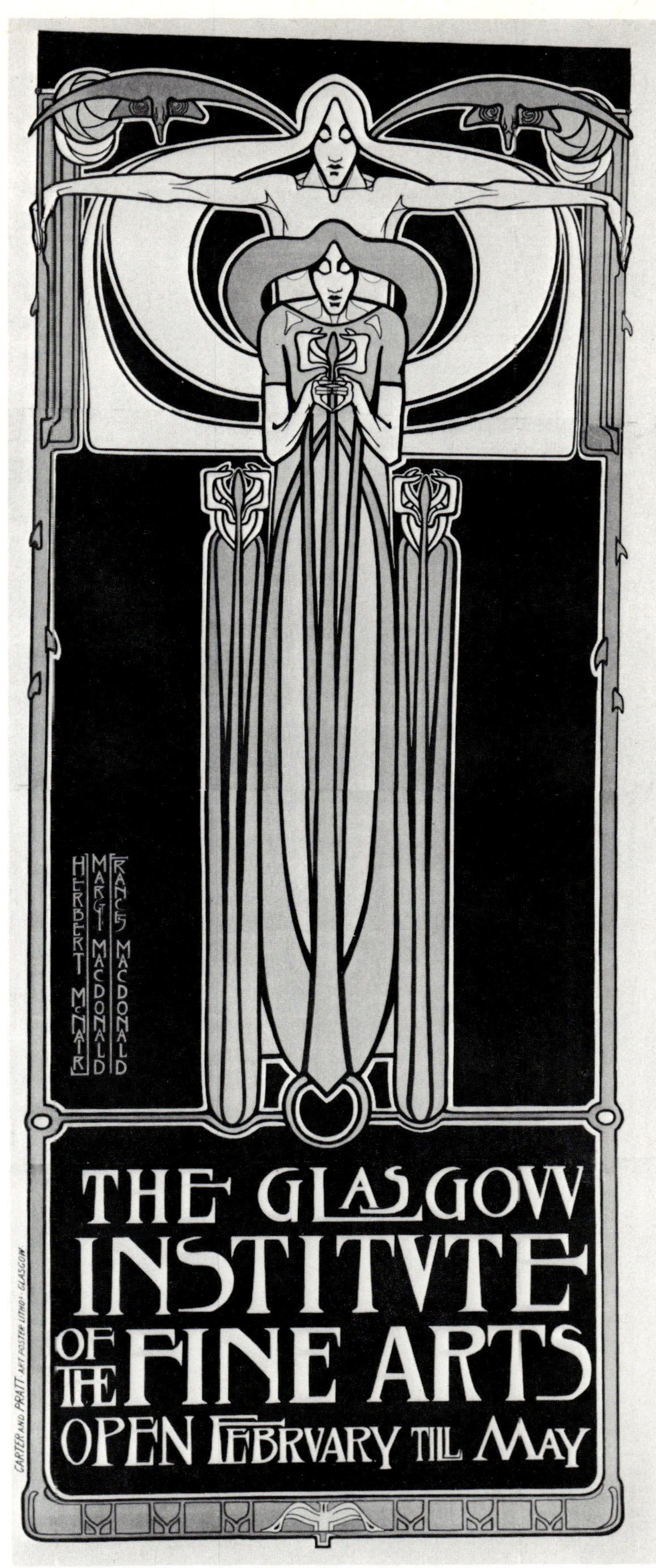


H. McNair, M. Macdonald & F. Macdonald
*Glasgow Institute of the Fine Arts* c 1896

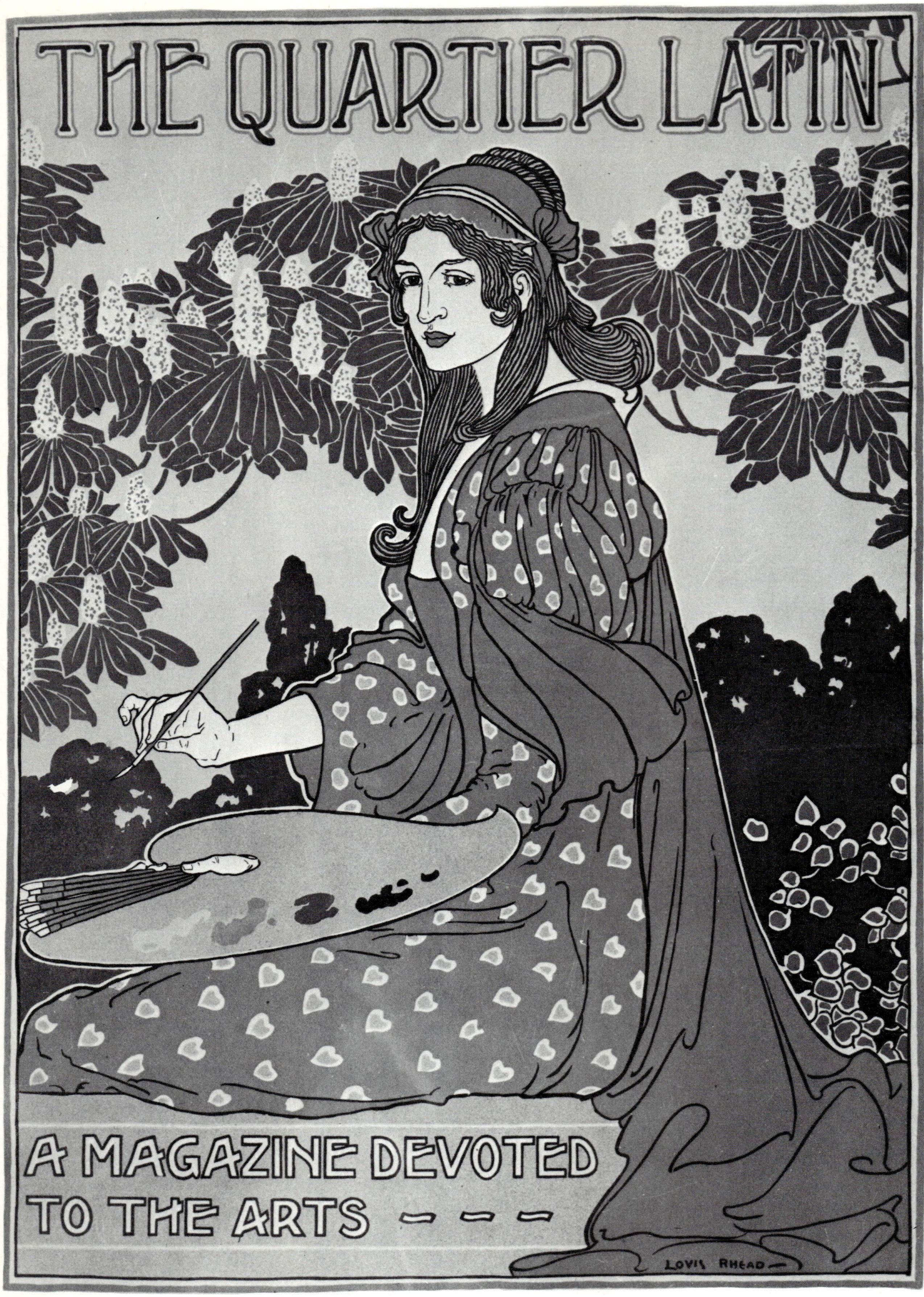


Louis Rhead
*Quartier Latin*

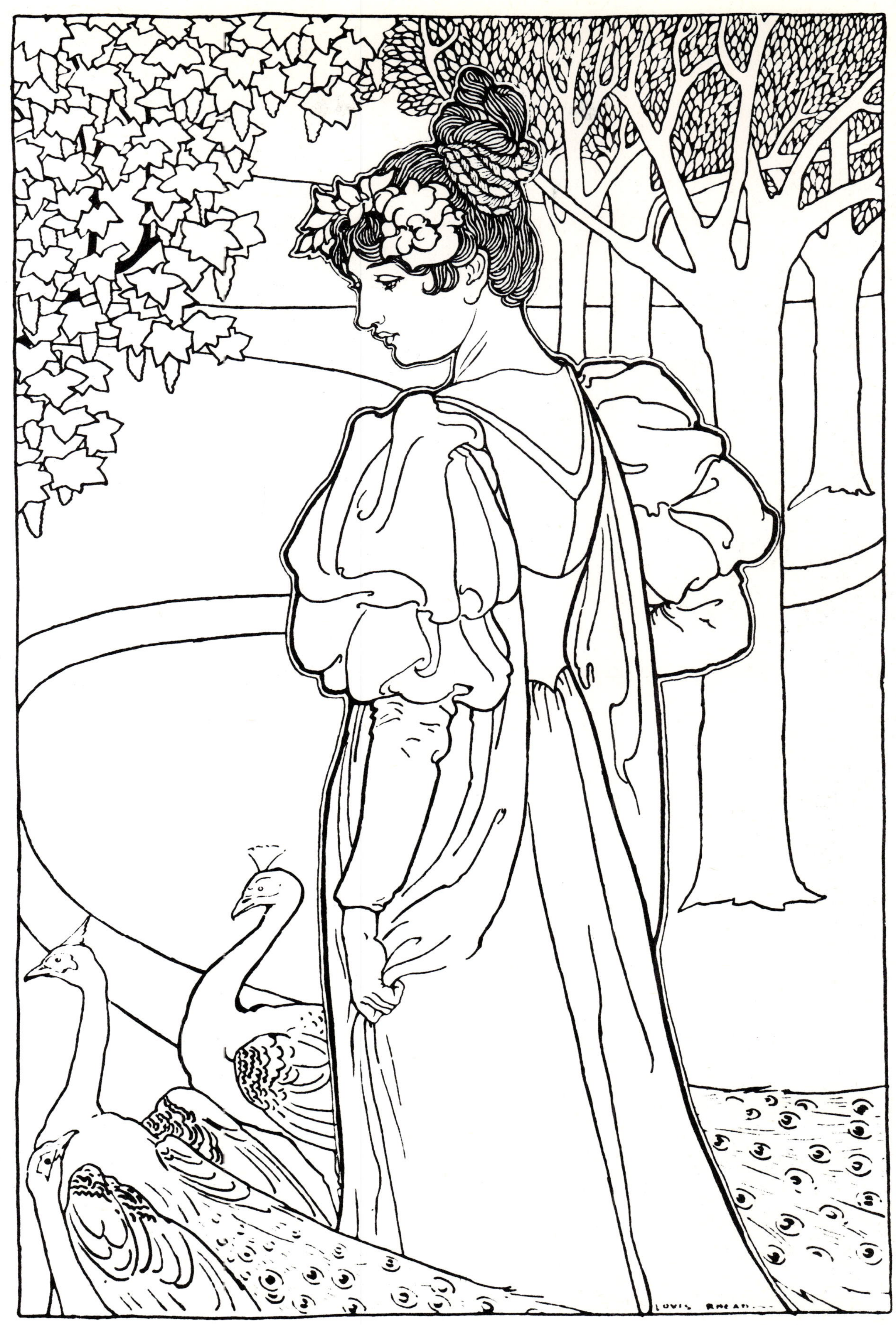


Louis Rhead
*L'Estampe moderne: La Femme au Paon* 1897

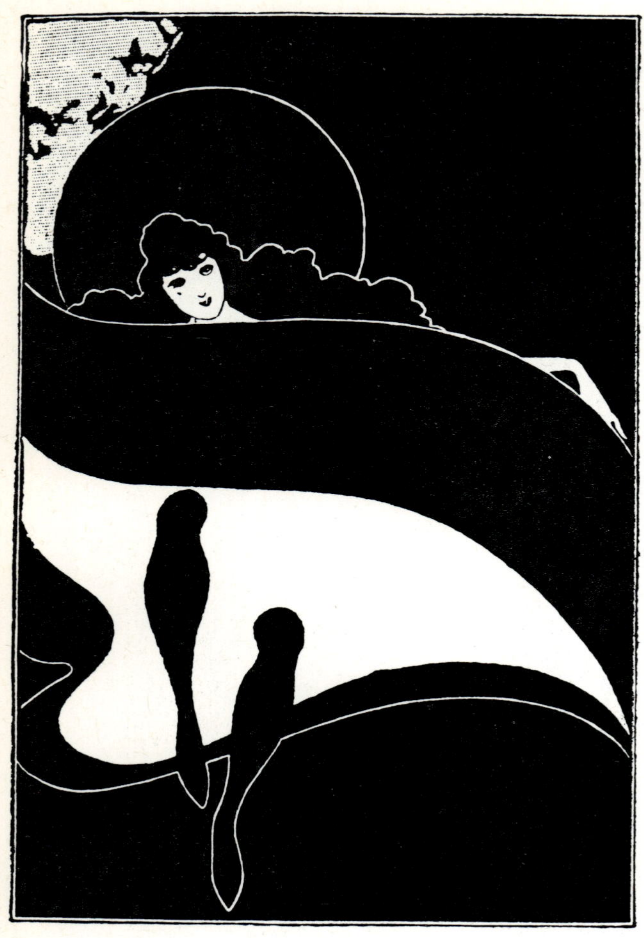

Will H. Bradley
*The Skirt Dancer* 1894

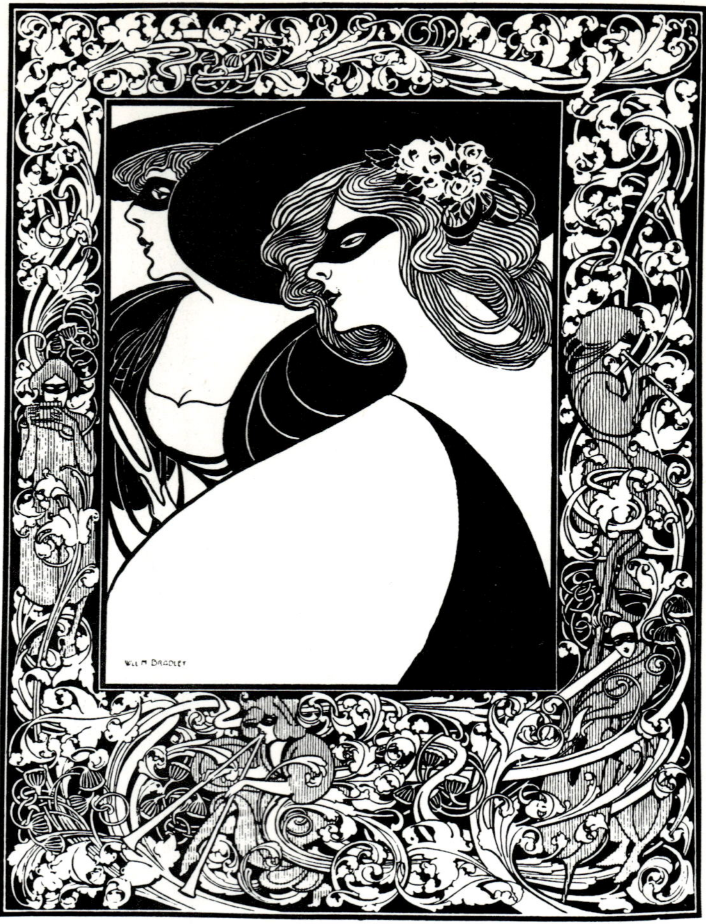



Will H. Bradley
*Chicago Sunday Tribune: Masquerade* 1895

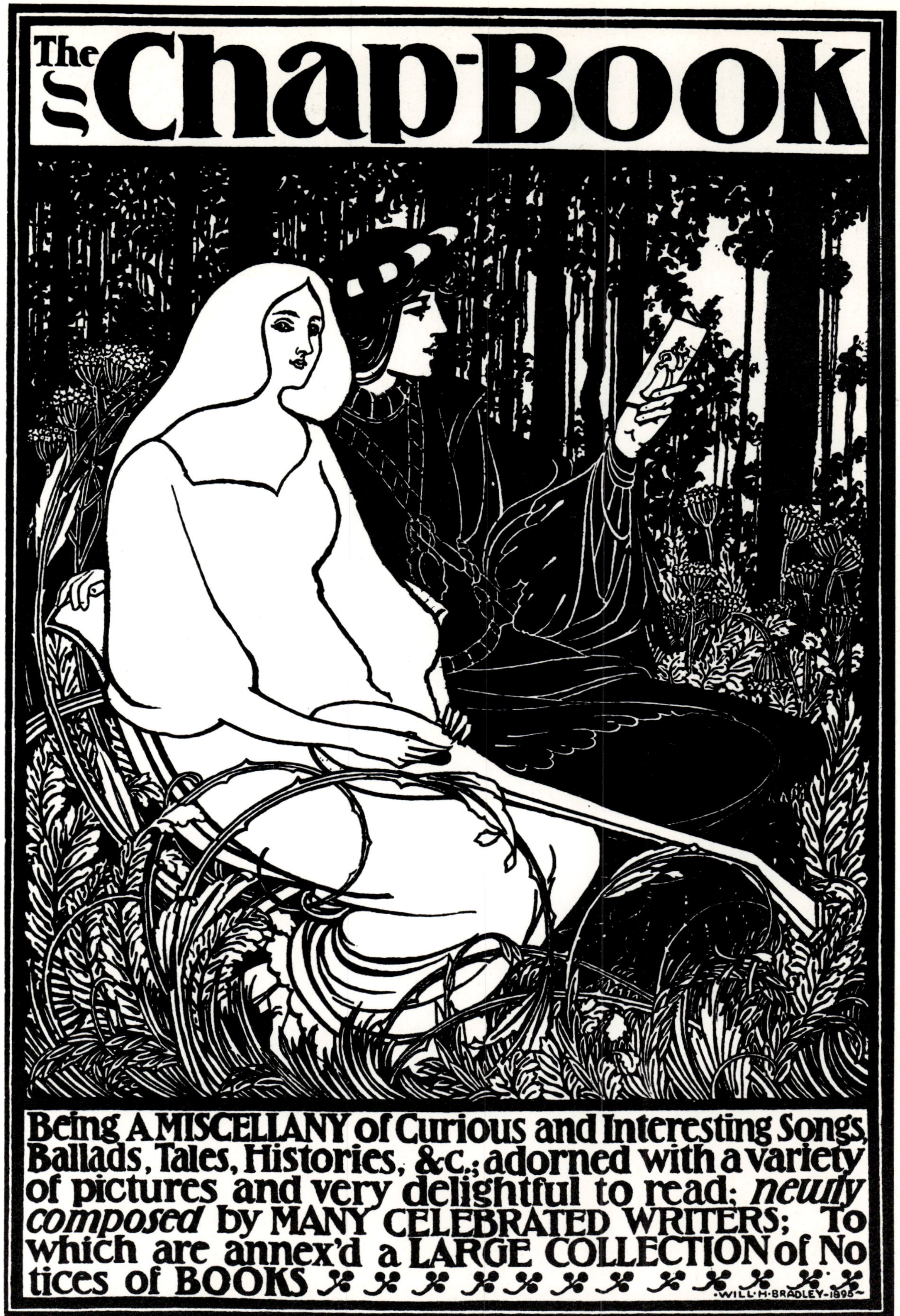


Will H. Bradley
*The Chap-Book: The Poet and his Lady* 1895

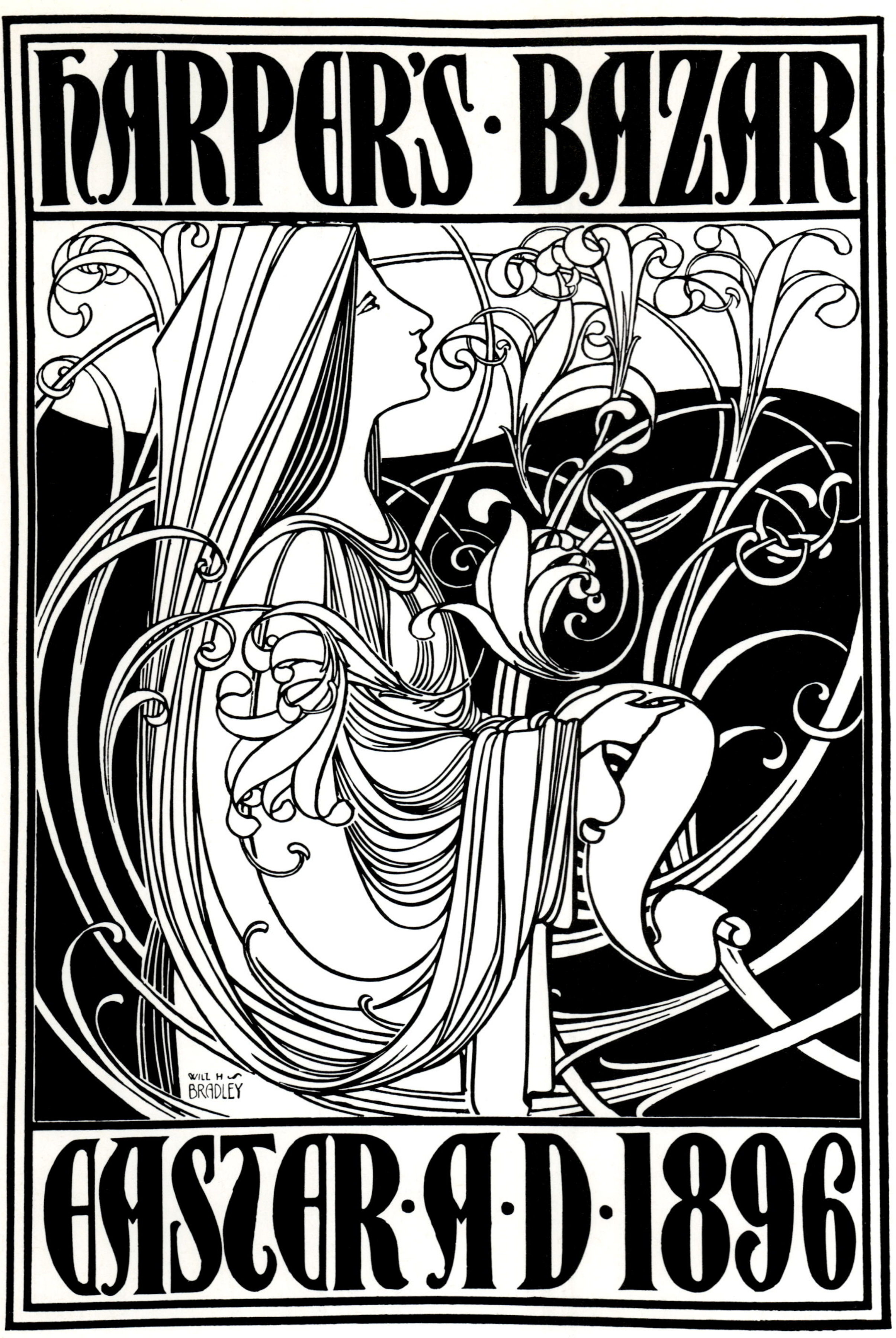


Will H. Bradley
*Harper's Bazaar*

# INDEX


A

Alastair . . . 66
Aman-Jean, Edmond-Francois . . . 27
Austen, John . . . 73

B

Bastard, E.M. . . . 29
Beardsley, Aubrey . . . 79, 80, 81, 82, 83
Berthon, Paul . . . 14, 15, 16, 17
Boano, G. . . . 68
Bonnard, Pierre . . . 8
Bradley, Will H. . . . 88, 92, 93, 94
Bussière, G. . . . 38

C

Christiansen, Hans . . . 61
Combaz, Gisbert . . . 58

E

Engels, Robert . . . 70
Evenpoel, Henri . . . 60

F

Feure, Georges de . . . 7, 22, 23, 45
Fidus . . . 67
Foäche . . . 37
French, Annie . . . 74

G

Grasset, Eugène . . . 18, 19, 20, 21, 35
Golay, Mary . . . 30, 31

H

Henning, Hans . . . 66
Hoffman, Josef . . . 69
Hohlwein, Ludwig . . . 10
Höppener, Hans . . . 67

J

Jones, A. Garth . . . 72

K

King, Jessie M. . . . 77, 78

L

Lang, Joseph Adolph . . . 76
Lenoir, Marcel . . . 48
List, Wilhelm . . . 63
Livemont, Privat . . . 35, 36, 39, 40, 41
Lucas, Hippolyte . . . 49

M

Macdonald, Frances . . . 89
Macdonald, Margaret . . . 89
Mackintosh, Charles Rennie . . . 84
Marie, Gustave . . . 39
Mariel, E. . . . 52
McNair, Herbert . . . 89
Melchers, Franz M. . . . 75
Meunier, Henri . . . 47
Moser, Kolo . . . 11, 12
Mucha, Alphonse Marie . . . 53, 54, 55, 56, 57

N

Nicholson, William . . . 71

O

Orazi, Manuel . . . 32, 33, 46

R

Ranson, Paul . . . 25, 26
Ranft, Richard . . . 34
Rhead, Louis . . . 86, 87, 90, 91
Rochegrosse, Georges . . . 13
Roubille, Alfred . . . 9, 24

S

Sattler, Josef . . . 85
Stolba, Leopold . . . 62

T

Tamagno . . . 28
Toorop, Jan . . . 2
Toulouse-Lautrec, Henri de . . . 50, 51

V

Vallotton, Félix . . . 42, 43, 44
Velde, Henry van de . . . 6, 10, 59
Vrieslander, John Jack . . . 64

W

Waroquier, Henri de . . . 34

Z

Zarth, Hans . . . 65